£29.99
(M)

Reconstructing Europe's trade and payments

Insights from Economic History
General editor: Nick Crafts

This series makes accessible major results from recent research in economic history, with an emphasis on issues of current importance. The books present an authoritative and objective view of the 'lessons of history' for the non-expert, while comprising essential reference material for the professional economic historian. The focus of the series is on issues in economic history that have contemporary relevance for policy makers and for economists wishing for a digest of key research results.

Barry Eichengreen

Reconstructing Europe's trade and payments

The European Payments Union

Manchester University Press

Copyright © Barry Eichengreen 1993

Published by Manchester University Press
Oxford Road, Manchester M13 9PL, UK

British Library Cataloguing-in-Publication Data
A catalogue record for this book is available from the British Library

ISBN 0 7190 4183 X *hardback*
       0 7190 4184 8 *paperback*

Photoset in Linotron Sabon by
Northern Phototypesetting Co Ltd., Bolton
Printed in Great Britain by
Biddles Ltd., Guildford and King's Lynn

Contents

Figures

Tables

Preface and acknowledgements

My interest in the European Payments Union dates back to my oral field exam in the Ph.D. program at Yale University, a memorable occasion (for the candidate if no one else) when I first met the late Robert Triffin, the EPU's architect. The topic's relevance to a series entitled *Insights from Economic History* should be obvious. At the time of writing, trade among the independent states of the former Soviet Union (the FSU) has undergone an alarming decline. The absence of a mechanism for settling transactions multilaterally is a major factor contributing to the problem. This has created nostalgia for the EPU, which provided such a successful basis for reconstructing Western Europe's trade following World War II. These policy concerns account in large part for the recent flurry of EPU-related research upon which this study builds.

As an economic historian my goal is not to give policy advice, however, but to understand the history. I argue that the EPU cannot be comprehended simply as a mechanism for multilateral clearing between contiguous countries seeking to eliminate the restrictive effects of bilateral trade agreements. Rather, the EPU was a very special arrangement designed to respond to the challenges and opportunities facing Western Europe after World War II. I have sought to situate the EPU in its historical context by describing the situation that arose in Western Europe following the war and to explain the sense in which the EPU was a logical response. Inevitably this leads to skepticism that an EPU-like arrangement would be appropriate today for the successor states of the Soviet Union, where the political and economic context is so very different. But perhaps this insight, such as it is, itself represents a modest contribution to the policy debate.

Many individuals and organizations helped with making this little book. Financial support was provided by the National Science Foundation (Economics Division) and by the Center for German and European Studies and the Institute of International Studies at the University of California at Berkeley. I began the research while visiting the International Finance Division of the Board of Governors of the Federal Reserve System and the Research Department of the International Monetary Fund. I completed it during a sabbatical year at the Institute for Advanced Study in Berlin, portions of which were also spent at the Institute for International Economic Studies in Stockholm and the Bank of France. I thank my hosts for their hospitality and their indulgence with my peripatetic ways.

Colleagues, students, friends and family contributed generously to the development of this research. Pamela Fox provided logistical support and prepared the index. Alan Winters kindly shared his data. Dan Eichengreen helped with translations. Edward Bernstein, Alec Cairncross, Herbert Giersch, Jacob Kaplan, Peter Kenen, Alan Milward, Jacques Polak, Albrecht Ritschl, Holger Schmieding, Pierre Sicsic and Paul Welfens provided much-valued comments. My thinking was clarified by conversations with Michael Burda, Susan Collins, Michael Jones and Charles Wyplosz. I elaborated some of the policy implications for an article in *Economic Policy*; for their input I thank its coeditor, David Begg, and my discussants, Stanley Fischer and Vittorio Grilli. Nick Crafts, academic editor of *Insights from Economic History*, is responsible for this monograph's appearance in that series. Francis Brooke of Manchester University Press saw it into print. Luisa Lambertini, Graham Schindler and Ansgar Rumler all provided sterling research assistance. Ansgar died tragically in an avalanche while skiing in the Austrian alps the very week final touches were being put on the manuscript. He will be missed by all who knew him.

Chapter 1

Introduction

The European Payments Union (EPU) is widely hailed as a critical step toward the restoration of free international trade and payments after World War II. From 1950 to 1958 the EPU promoted multilateral settlements, encouraged the removal of trade barriers, and cemented the stability of exchange rates. Participating countries agreed to accept the currency of any other member in payment for exports, instantly unsnarling the suffocating tangle of bilateral agreements upon which Europe's trade had been based.[1] Deficit countries were provided credits to finance temporary trade imbalances, obviating the need to restrict imports and potentially, employment and growth. Under the beneficent influence of this system, intra-European trade expanded vigorously, helping to fuel the postwar resurgence of the Western European economy.

All this has the appearance of a remarkable success, which is the way the EPU is typically portrayed. Yet in addition to its advantages, the EPU may have also had significant costs. The return to current account convertibility following World War II was delayed for nearly fifteen years. A transitional payments scheme designed to last for two years persisted for nearly nine. Participating countries were permitted to discriminate in one another's favor and against other countries, notably the

United States, creating scope for trade diversion as well as trade creation. By insulating European producers from international markets, the EPU could have allowed domestic prices to deviate from international prices, distorting the allocation of resources. By impeding the repatriation of foreign earnings, the EPU could have discouraged the American investment that Europe so desperately required.

These possibilities are hardly mentioned in recent scholarship.[2] The EPU, as two of the leading contributors to the literature observe, is probably 'the only multilateral institution created after World War II whose claim to unmitigated success has gone unchallenged.'[3]

The glowing portrait that so dominates the literature may be colored by the fact that the only two substantial analyses of the EPU's operation were written, respectively, by the architect of the system (Triffin 1957) and by two members of its managing board (Kaplan and Schleiminger 1989).[4] The only places where questions about the EPU's advisability have been raised, even in passing, are Friedman (1953), Berg and Sachs (1992) and Giersch *et al.* (1992).[5] None of them challenges the notion that the EPU was preferable to the agreements that forced European countries to balance their trade bilaterally immediately after World War II. But, indirectly at least, each raises the question of whether the EPU was a less desirable response to bilateralism than a return to current account convertibility in the early 1950s.[6] In so doing they imply that favorable evaluations of the EPU may reflect a failure to specify the appropriate counterfactual, which included convertibility as well as bilateralism.[7]

These authors do not follow up their skepticism with a systematic analysis of the viability of these other options nor weigh them against the EPU. That is my goal in the present study. It should be obvious why we would want such an analysis and comparison. Interest in the EPU has been heightened by the collapse of the Council on Mutual Economic Assistance (CMEA) and disintegration of the USSR, which disrupted trade among the Soviet Union's successor states. The volume of intra-FSU trade is thought to have declined by more than 50 per cent between 1990 and 1992 and by as much as 30 per cent in 1992 alone.[8] Shortages of consumer goods, energy and industrial materials prompted governments to slap controls on exports. Chaos in the financial system deterred potential exporters who did not know how, when or even whether they would be paid. Historical enmities among the successor states resurfaced, leading them to sever long-standing trade relationships. Perhaps most importantly, there was no mechanism for settling inter-republican transactions multilaterally. There was no way, in other words, to use receipts from exporting to one republic to finance imports from another.

The parallels with Western Europe after World War II are striking. Much like the FSU, Europe after the war was burdened with heavily distorted trade and production patterns, widespread controls, and repressed and open inflation. Much like the trade of the FSU, Europe's trade was based on a restrictive network of bilateral agreements. As in the FSU, the adjustment of trade in postwar Europe lagged behind the adjustment of production.

The success with which the countries of what became the European Community subsequently rebuilt their international transactions has led several authors to recommend an EPU-style payments union for the FSU.[9] Others, however, have questioned the viability of an EPU-like arrangement and argued that a payments union is an inferior alternative to convertibility.[10]

These are the issues taken up in the present monograph. Chapter 2 recounts the payments problems of the immediate post-World War II period, describes the structure of the EPU, and analyzes the evolution of Europe's trade. Chapter 3 presents contemporary explanations for the decision to adopt the EPU and to reject convertibility as unworkable. These include the unresponsiveness of imports and exports to exchange rates, the inadequacy of international reserves, and the existence monetary overhangs. This chapter then goes on to assess the validity of these explanations. The question lurking behind the scenes is whether the EPU was necessary – that is, whether convertibility was also viable at the beginning of the 1950s. Strikingly, the standard prerequisites for current account convertibility appear to have been satisfied by every EPU participant but Ireland and the United Kingdom from the beginning of the decade. Even the UK's abortive attempt to restore convertibility in 1947, considered in Chapter 4, serves as proof by counter-example and in this sense supports the conclusion.

This might be thought to mark the end of the story, the message being that the EPU was a mistake adopted in lieu of the superior alternative of convertibility. But this, I suggest, was not the case. European policy-makers, far from misguided, had subtler reasons for opting for the EPU. I advance an interpretation of Europe's postwar payments scheme in Chapter 5 that focuses on considerations different from those emphasized by authors concerned exclusively with international trade and payments. A critical function of the EPU, I suggest, was to help seal the domestic and international bargains upon which the post-World War II generation of European economic growth was based. Domestically, growth required stabilization, and stabilization required consensus on income distribution. The EPU moderated the sacrifices necessary to bring this consensus about. By turning the terms of trade in Europe's favor, it minimized the concessions in terms of living standards required for a distributional settlement.

Once agreement was reached, however, it had to be sustained. The EPU, as a concommitant of the 'social market economy' that was at the heart of the postwar settlement, helped to do just that. It was one of the web of institutional arrangements that 'locked in' the domestic distributional compact.

Internationally, the postwar settlement involved a commitment to trade and European integration. For countries to restructure their economies along export-oriented lines, they had to be convinced that their neighbors embraced the same commitment. Here the EPU acted as an institutional exit barrier lending credibility to the commitment to trade and integration.

These advantages of the EPU dominated only insofar as they were not swamped by distortions associated with the operation of inconvertible currencies and regional payments schemes. Chapter 6 therefore considers whether the EPU spawned trade and price distortions and hampered foreign borrowing. I analyze trade creation and trade diversion, differences in relative price structures in EPU countries and the rest of the world, and differences in access to foreign capital. Finding little evidence of trade, relative-price and capital-market distortions, I attempt to identify the special features of the EPU that successfully minimized the distortions typically afflicting payments union schemes.

Chapter 7 returns to the implications for the successor states of the former Soviet Union. Interpreting the EPU as a prerequisite for the social market economy and a device for reconciling prevailing living standards with balanced extra-European trade offers a suggestive precedent for FSU countries in which income distribution remains a hotly-contested issue. Despite the need for a distributional settlement akin to that achieved in post-World War II Western Europe, however, it seems unlikely that a payments union scheme could play as important a role in consummating it in the FSU today as in Western Europe half a century ago. The other elements of a social compact are not yet in place. Given their lack of market power, the terms-of-trade gains that might minimize the sacrifices entailed in its negotiation are not available to the former-Soviet republics.

Could a payments union agreement nudge the independent states of the former Soviet Union toward greater intra-regional trade and economic integration, in the same way that the EPU encouraged Western European nations to expand their intra-European trade and helped lay the basis for the European Economic Community? A credible commitment to liberalize intra-FSU trade and the creation of an international institution with monitoring and enforcement capabilities to deter the participants from reneging on their pact would give the FSU countries the confidence required to restructure their economies along export-oriented lines, enabling them to exploit their comparative advantages and at the same time to reap the scale economies characteristic of the old centrally-planned regime. But after World War II the commitment to trade and economic integration in Western Europe was locked in by the creation of institutions whose short-run goal was stronger economic links and whose ultimate objective, at least in the eyes of some, was political unification. These are precisely the kind of ties that the republics of the former Soviet Union are seeking to move away from today. It seems implausible, therefore, that a payments union scheme could provide part of a broader integrationist framework that locked in a durable international settlement among the former-Soviet republics.

Given the profound differences in circumstances between Western Europe after World War II and the former Soviet Union today, it is logical that arrangements for regulating intra-regional trade and payments should take a different form. But even if the EPU is not an appropriate model for the former Soviet Union, post-war experience nonetheless has important implications for current policy in that part of the world. If the countries of the FSU do opt for some kind of payments union scheme, it will be important to emulate the EPU by designing it to minimize trade diversion, relative price distortions, and impediments to foreign borrowing. Moreover, it will be essential to defer the provision of credit-based settlements for clearing union participants in deficit until after macroeconomic stabilization has occurred. To do otherwise would simply reward the countries running the worst policies and doom any FSU clearing union to the same sad fate as the abortive predecessors of the European Payments Union.

Notes

1 Where no qualifier is used, Europe should be taken as referring to Western Europe.
2 See Kindleberger (1984), Tew (1988) and Kenen (1991) for important contributions.
3 Kaplan and Schleiminger (1989), p. 1.
4 Gunther Schleiminger was Alternate German Member of the Managing Board and Chairman of the Board of Alternates. Jacob J. Kaplan was US representative to the Managing Board. Their book was commissioned by the Bank for International Settlements, the EPU's financial agent.

5 This statement is true at least of the English language literature. In addition, German scholars such as Wilhelm Röpke and liberal politicians such as Ludwig Erhard criticized the EPU as discriminatory. See Erhard (1954). There is an irony in Erhard's skepticism about the EPU, given the benefits he is alleged to have derived from it (see Chapter 2).

6 Friedman has been misinterpreted – given his choice of title, understandably – as making a case for flexible exchange rates rather than currency convertibility. Yet his article was originally written in 1950 as a critique of the EPU. The essence of its argument, as Berg and Sachs note, is for convertibility at whatever exchange rate renders it viable, including a flexible one. This is a point to which I return in Chapter 3. It is important in this connection to distinguish two meanings of convertibility. In the literature on the gold standard (and the gold exchange standard of the 1920s), the term refers to the convertibility of domestic currency into gold (and thereby into other convertible currencies) at a fixed price. In the literature on subsequent periods, it refers to the convertibility of the domestic currency into foreign currencies at the currently prevailing market price. Hence convertibility is consistent with floating exchange rates. The literature on these more recent periods also distinguishes types of convertibility according to the purposes for which the authorities will permit domestic currency to be converted into foreign exchange. 'Current account convertibility' refers to a regime under which conversion is permitted only for current account transactions. Since current account convertibility was reinstituted at the end of 1958 and was the obvious alternative to the EPU, except where otherwise noted, 'convertibility' refers to 'current account convertibility' wherever it appears.

7 Triffin (1957), for example, simply asserts that an early restoration of convertibility was not viable, and contrasts the EPU with the alternative of bilateralism alone.

8 The unreliability of published figures, due to disarray in the relevant statistical bureaus of newly-independent republics and to widespread smuggling, forces us to rely on informal estimates. Those in the text are due to Michalopoulis and Tarr (1993) and Gros (1993).

9 See for example Dornbusch (1992) and Williamson (1992). Previous proposals along similar lines for Eastern Europe include United Nations (1990), Ethier (1990), Lavigne (1990), Soros (1990), Buchheim (1990) and van Brabant (1990).

10 The limited applicability of EPU-like schemes under present circum-

stances is emphasized by Kenen (1991) and Polak (1991), among others. Berg and Sachs (1992) argue strongly for the superiority of current account convertibility.

Chapter 2

Background

The nations of Western Europe emerged from World War II with their economies in disarray but their capacity for growth intact. War-related damage and dislocation were extensive. Mines had been flooded, factories dismantled by retreating armies. Germany was divided into four zones of Allied occupation and inundated with refugees from the East. Strategic bombing had knocked out roads, bridges, railways and a significant portion of the housing stock. Long-standing trade relations were disrupted.

All this posed formidable problems for those seeking to resume business as usual. Decentralized market economies are comprised of an an intricate web of interdependent sectors and activities. Disruption of one sector or activity can reverberate through the economy. And Western European economies experienced a barrage of such disruptions in the aftermath of the war. Businesses could not operate because damage to the transport system prevented them from shipping materials to the factory and products to the market. Banks balked at lending to firms whose ability to acquire materials and market their products remained uncertain. Faced with such problems, employers hesitated to rehire demobilized servicemen, which in turn limited the level of final demand. These problems, and not wartime destruction of industrial capacity *per se*, depressed industrial production in the immediate post-war months to less than 20 per cent of pre-war levels in Italy and Germany and 30–40 per cent in Belgium and France.

Among the most debilitating problems was the collapse of Europe's trade. Imported foodstuffs, raw materials and capital goods were desperately needed for sustenance and reconstruction. But given the scarcity of international reserves and credits, Europe's capacity to import was limited by its ability to export. Its ability to export was constrained in turn by the scarcity of imported inputs, in a classic Catch-22 situation.

Trade and balance-of-payments adjustment before the EPU

At the root of this problem was the dollar shortage. America was the only source of much of the capital equipment required for reconstruction and of intermediate inputs like cotton and coal needed for the utilization of existing capacity.[1] As shown in Table 1, Europe ran a current account deficit with the United States of $5.6 billion dollars in 1947, $3.4 billion in 1948 and $3.2 billion in 1949.[2] Europe still had limited amounts of dollars and gold with which it could finance imports from the rest of the world. The Marshall Plan and other forms of US aid also helped to relax the external constraint. But throughout Western Europe, excess demand for imports from countries demanding hard currency in settlement – the so-called dollar area – remained pervasive.

A natural question is why Europe did not finance more of these imports by increasing its exports of manufactures and other goods. By exporting more to the Western hemisphere, European countries could have eliminated their dollar deficits.

Table 1 The financing of Europe's overseas deficit
(Billions of current dollars)

	1947 United States	1947 other overseas countries	1947 total	1948 United States	1948 other overseas countries	1948 total	1949 United States	1949 other overseas countries	1949 total	1950 United States	1950 other overseas countries	1950 total
I Balance on goods and services and other transactions making up the deficit:												
Balance on goods and services	−5.6	−1.8	−7.4	−3.4	−1.5	−4.9	−3.2	−0.6	−3.8	−1.6	−0.9	−2.5
Private donations	0.4	−	0.4	0.4	−0.1	0.3	0.4	−0.1	0.3	−0.3	−0.1	0.2
Private capital movements	0.3	−1.1	−0.8	0.2	−0.1	0.1	−0.1	−0.4	−0.5	−0.1	−0.1	−0.2
Special official financing (debt settlements, specific investment projects, etc.)	−0.6	−0.1	−0.7	−0.2	−0.3	−0.5	0.2	−0.4	−0.2	0.5	−0.3	0.2
Total deficit to be financed:												
Unadjusted	−5.5	−3.0	−8.5	−3.0	−2.0	−5.0	−2.7	−1.5	−4.2	−0.9	−1.4	−2.3
Adjustments	−0.3	−	−0.3	−	−0.1	−0.1	−0.2	0.7	0.5	−0.1	0.5	0.4
Adjusted	−5.8	−3.0	−8.8	−3.0	−2.1	−5.1	−2.9	−0.8	−3.7	−1.0	−0.9	−1.9
II Official financing of a compensatory nature:												
Government grants	1.0	−	1.0	3.2	−	3.2	4.1	−	4.1	2.7	−	2.7
Long-term capital movement	3.8	0.9	4.7	1.1	0.5	1.6	0.7	−0.5	0.2	0.2	−	0.2
Financing by international institutions	1.1	0.1	1.2	0.3	−	0.3	−	−	−	−	−	−
Movement in sterling balances	−	−0.6	−0.6	−	−0.2	−0.2	−0.1	−0.5	−0.5	−0.2	0.9	0.9
Movement in US dollar balances	0.8	−	0.8	−0.3	−	−0.3	0.2	−	−0.1	−0.2	−	−0.2
Gold movement	1.9	−0.2	1.7	0.9	−0.4	0.5	−	−0.2	−	−1.3	−0.4	−1.7
Total compensatory official financing	8.6	0.2	8.8	5.2	−0.1	5.1	4.9	−1.2	3.7	1.4	0.5	1.9
III Multilateral settlements in U.S. dollars:												
ERP reimbursement for European purchases outside the United States	−	−	−	−0.8	0.8	−	−1.0	1.0	−	−0.7	0.7	−
Other dollar settlements by European countries outside the United States	−2.8	2.8	−	−1.4	1.4	−	−1.0	1.0	−	0.3	−0.3	−
Total multilateral settlements in US dollars	−2.8	2.8	−	−2.2	2.2	−	−2.0	2.0	−	−0.4	0.4	−

Source: United Nations (1950), p. 116; United Nations (1951), p. 118.

Part of the explanation, as already noted, is that imported inputs from the United States were first needed to restart production, and exports could only follow with a lag. Another obstacle was real overvaluation. Table 2 shows, for various European countries, average hourly earnings in industry, expressed in US dollars, as a percentage of 1938 levels. Adjusting for changes in labor productivity in industry, as in the last three columns of the table, shows relative labor costs in Europe to have increased significantly since before the war. Output per worker in US industry rose by some 30 per cent; over much of Europe it rose hardly at all. High labor costs translated into high prices. Compared to 1938, the unit values of US exports were 97 per cent higher in 1947, 107 per cent higher in 1948; corresponding figures for Europe's trade with non-European countries were 112 and 121 per cent.[3] Trade deficits *vis-à-vis* the United States were the inevitable result.

To maximize the availability of hard currency that might be used to purchase from the dollar area the imports to which they attached priority, European countries restricted their imports from the rest of Europe to the value of their receipts in each European trading partner's currency. As William Diebold summarized the situation

'Most European currencies were inconvertible: they could not be exchanged for other currencies except with official permission and for limited purposes (unless they were exchanged illegally, at black-market rates). Only a few European countries were willing to hold substantial balances of another's currency for any length of time. In general if a country could not use these soft currencies for essential imports, it tried to get gold or dollars for them. At the same time each country tried as often as it could to sell its own products for dollars, either by directing its exports to hard currency countries or, if the goods it had to offer were scarce

Table 2   Movement in industrial wages and labor costs of European
countries in terms of corresponding movements in the United States
Index numbers − 1938 = 100
Adjusted for changes in exchange rates

Country	Average hourly earnings			Average hourly earnings adjusted for changes in labor productivity		
	1946	1947	1948	1946	1947	1948
Austria	28	44	68	92	144	162
Belgium	116	120	−	156	172	−
Bulgaria	153	150	−	−	214	−
Czechoslovakia[b]	101	93	86	−	135	113
Denmark	97	91	89	150	128	118
Finland	126	157	189	184	202	213
France	77	96	−	124	138	−
Italy	86	82	81	211	154	139
Ireland	65	68	66	84	92	81
Netherlands[c]	78	74	71	143	125	109
Norway	79	78	−	125	119	−
Sweden	97	108	108	113	124	121
United Kingdom	91	88	86	117	111	101

Notes:
[a] Base of index numbers: 1936–1938.
[b] Base of index numbers: 1939.
[c] Base of index numbers: 1938/1939.

Source: United Nations (1949), p.107.

enough, by insisting that European customers pay for them in
dollars.[4]

This was the genesis of the bilateral agreements upon which
intra-European trade was organized following World War II.
In the late 1940s, intra-European trade was dominated by
some 200 such arrangements. Contracting governments
agreed to lists of commodities for which they would issue
import licenses up to agreed limits. The more restrictive
agreements pre-set prices as well as quantities in order to
guarantee bilateral balance on a continuous basis. With trade
balanced bilaterally, the currency in which settlements might

be effected was rendered irrelevant. In cases where prices or quantities could vary, temporary deficits could result. These were financed by the partner in surplus up to a specified ceiling or swing. The bilateral agreements concluded by Belgium, Switzerland and the Allied Zone of Occupation in Germany required settlement in gold or dollars when credit lines were exhausted or the agreement expired. (Belgium and Switzerland anticipated being in substantial surplus with their European trading partners following World War II, while the United States expected to find itself underwriting German production and trade; hence their insistence on hard-currency settlements.) In other cases, notably those of the UK and the Scandinavian countries, when cumulative net bilateral deficits exceeded the ceiling, the bilateral agreement might be renegotiated and the ceiling raised.[5]

In light of its association with German economic policy in the 1930s, bilateralism had negative connotations. But as Diebold (1952) and Triffin (1957) point out, in the aftermath of World War II the alternative to bilateralism was autarchy. Because they included mutual credit facilities, bilateral agreements were a positive step toward rebuilding Europe's trade. Bilateral credit lines were the grease that allowed the wheels of intra-European trade to start turning again. Even the Bank for International Settlements, not one that would normally trumpet the virtues of bilateral agreements, praised their operation in 1948,

> In 1945, during the first phase of their operation, the payments agreements had, indeed, the great virtue of making commercial relations possible on a scale that could not otherwise have been achieved; they got goods moving between countries which, in many cases, had been physically severed from each other for many years. They helped to establish a

uniform and smoothly working payments mechanism with a series of reasonable and consistent exchange rates and with relatively flexible controls. They made it possible to economize on the use of gold and international exchange and to develop export capacities. As a result, there was a widespread revival of intra-European trade after the barren years of war.[6]

Reciprocal overdraft rights were premised on the idea that surpluses and deficits would alternate. A country in deficit in one period might be in surplus the next, allowing any credits it had drawn to be repaid. Experience demonstrated, however, that some countries tended toward persistent deficit, others toward persistent surplus. Once credit ceilings were reached, additional credits were not forthcoming. And once credits were exhausted, bilateral clearing became increasingly constraining. As United Nations experts commented in 1950,

> In the period immediately following the war, bilateral agreements permitted the rapid rebuilding of trade relations . . . This was partly made possible by the substantial credits granted by the main creditor countries which obviated the necessity for the close bilateral balancing of trade. By 1948, the exhaustion of these facilities and the unwillingness to grant further credits had caused a fairly widespread tightening of payments and renewed emphasis on balancing in bilateral relations.[7]

Several factors contributed to this situation. The growth of trade rendered existing credit facilities increasingly inadequate. Ability to meet consumption and investment demands out of domestic capacity recovered more quickly in some countries than others. Monetary and fiscal stabilization was completed early in some places, late in others. The UK, whose productive capacity remained largely intact, initially ran substantial surpluses in its European trade. By the end of 1947, the importing countries had largely exhausted their spare margin of gold and dollar reserves. Since the UK demanded hard currency in settlement, they were forced to limit imports from Britain to the value of their exports to that market. With the early recovery of its steel industry, Belgium too ran substantial trade surpluses against the rest of Europe and similarly found her market access restricted once European partners refused to part with gold and foreign exchange. At the end of 1947, France exceeded her credit ceiling with Belgium and was compelled for a time to cease importing from that country.[8] Even the UK, which was in surplus with the continent as a whole, was in deficit with Belgium and in March 1948 negotiated an agreement under which accounts were to be balanced and sterling transfers from other countries to Belgium were restricted. The Netherlands ran deficits with Belgium in excess of bilateral ceilings and was forced to drastically curtail imports in the second half of 1948. Sweden and Switzerland initially ran trade deficits against the rest of Europe but grew increasingly concerned over their loss of reserves as the period progressed. Sweden placed a temporary ban on further imports from Belgium in March of 1948. Switzerland revoked provisions of bilateral agreements with Denmark and Austria that had allowed these countries relatively free use of their Swiss franc earnings for purchases in third countries. The trade of both Sweden and Switzerland with the rest of the European continent declined significantly in the first part of 1949.[9]

Thus, following a grace period in which swing credits financed the recovery of intra-European trade, credit facilities were exhausted and bilateral balancing agreements bound. Downward pressure was placed on the entire network of Europe's trade.

The failure of pre-EPU clearing initiatives

The obvious solution to these problems was a multilateral clearing agreement. If for example Denmark could use its surplus vis-à-vis Sweden to finance its deficit vis-à-vis France, many of the restrictive effects of bilateralism could be relaxed. (If Sweden was in surplus with France, it could in turn offset that against its deficit with Denmark, leaving France no better or worse off.) Europe's dollar deficit would remain, but intra-European trade would be stimulated.

Beginning in 1947, a number of EPU-like initiatives were attempted with the goal of relaxing the restrictive effects of bilateral agreements. None had more than a marginal impact. In the absence of inflation stabilization, surplus countries hesitated to agree to a mechanism that featured credits. Double-digit inflation persisted in France and Greece, and monetary reform had not yet clearly eliminated the potential for inflation in Germany and Austria. Such countries might quickly absorb whatever credits were contributed by the participants as a group, which was unattractive to those who had done the most to stabilize their economies. The American economist John H. Williams put his finger on the point in 1949 when he wrote,

> The main road to viability for France is through correction of inflation, and the chief question to be asked of the French program is whether the corrective measures outlined will be adequate and will be feasible. Until an answer is given, inflation constitutes a threat not only to viability for France, but to the success of the entire E.C.A. program. While it lasts, French imports will remain abnormally high and exports abnormally low; the flight of capital, both externally and into hoarding at home, will continue; and France will threaten to divert increasingly to herself E.C.A. aid which should go to others.[10]

An early attempt at multilateral clearing took place in November 1947, when Belgium, Luxembourg, the Netherlands, France and Italy concluded the First Agreement on Multilateral Monetary Compensation. They sought to offset debts they had incurred through the operation of a bilateral agreement with one country against assets they had acquired through the operation of another. These operations were however limited to reductions in existing credit and debit balances; offsetting operations that would have reduced a country's debt against one partner by increasing its debt against another were not permitted.[11] No new credits were provided, in other words.

The absence of credits and the limited scope of the agreement proved debilitating. The Netherlands had a trade balance with every other party to the agreement, Italy a surplus. This left neither country any scope for cancelling liabilities multilaterally. At the end of December 1947, by which time $762.1 million in bilateral balances were outstanding, only $1.7 million had actually been offset.[12] Only $5 million in claims had been cancelled by the time the 1947–48 agreement expired. Nor was any 'substantial progress in the relaxation of discriminatory trade restrictions . . . made as a result of this Agreement.'[13] Even the Bank for International Settlements, an enthusiast of the initiative, had to admit that the results were 'limited.'[14]

A second attempt in October 1948, the so-called Agreement for Intra-European Payments and Compensations, committed all OEEC (Organization for European Economic Cooperation) countries to multilateral debt cancellation. This agreement was renewed in June 1949 and ran until the EPU was inaugurated in July 1950. Again, no credits were provided. Like its predecessor, this agreement made only a small contribution to financing Europe's trade. Only a fraction of the gross deficits incurred under the provisions of existing bilateral agreements were canceled multilaterally under the 1948–50 scheme. Triffin concludes that only about four per cent of the claims that would have been eliminated under a system of full and automatic multilateral compensation applying to all of Western Europe like that adopted later under the EPU was actually cleared under the provisions of the 1947–8 and 1948–50 agreements.[15]

Some relief was provided by the Marshall Plan (formally, the Economic Recovery Program, or ERP) in mid-1948. Not having to scramble quite so desperately for dollars, the recipients of Marshall aid could devote more hard currency to intra-European settlements. Moreover, the Economic Cooperation Administration (or ECA, which administered the Marshall Plan) authorized procurement authorizations for purchases within Europe. Rather than tying US grants to purchases of US exports, the ECA allowed the recipient to use the funds to purchase goods from third parties, including other aid recipients. Authorization for off-shore purchasing, as this practice was known, was especially important during the early months of the Marshall Plan. But the demand for imports of US goods remained insatiable. Procurement in participating ERP countries totalled less than $250 million in the final three quarters of 1948. This was perhaps one-fifteenth of contemporaneous Marshall aid and only three per cent of the value of intra-European trade. Governments still had to worry about intra-European trade deficits which threatened to deplete their dollar reserves. Bilateral restrictions were maintained.

The slow recovery of intra-European trade, compounded by the failure of the recipients to use their Marshall aid to finance imports from other European countries, frustrated American officials who saw trade and economic integration as the only reliable guarantors of a durable peace. Reinforcing their concern were the importance of trade to the US economy, the danger that a Europe which turned away from multi-lateralism might provide only limited access for US exports, and the failure of negotiations to establish an international trade organization.

US authorities sought to push Europe toward multi-lateralism by mandating the use of Marshall aid for intra-European settlements. Starting in October 1948, three months after the Marshall Plan came into operation, nations in surplus in intra-European trade were extended US grants, known as 'conditional aid,' which they were required to pass along in the form of credits (or 'drawing rights') to European nations in deficit. 'Conditional aid' was an ironic name, for the transfer was effectively unconditional: each country's total transfer appears to have been effectively decided before the intra-European payments plan was drawn up, and the US simply instructed recipient countries to transfer a portion of what they received to other recipients in the form of drawing rights.[16] Under the provisions of this so-called 'Little Marshall Plan,' deficit countries received drawing rights sufficient to cover a portion of their European deficits.

Allocating conditional aid and drawing rights prior to the advent of the deficits they were designed to finance gave rise to predictable problems. When forecasts erred seriously, the limits on existing clearing agreements might bind imme-diately.'The functioning of the system,' as Triffin put it, 'appears to have been as unpredictable and haphazard as that of the better known Monte Carlo roulette.'[17] Drawing rights were used to finance bilateral deficits on a monthly basis rather than cumulatively once deficits exceeded a specified threshold (as under the EPU); consequently they supported less trade. Drawing rights were extended on a bilateral basis; they could be wasted when extended to countries already receiving drawing rights from other participating countries. Only after considerable delay were deficit countries authorized to use up to twenty-five per cent of the drawing rights they received from one European trade partner to finance trade with another. Moreover, all bilateral drawing rights had to be used before recourse could be had to multilateral drawing rights. This perpetuated 'the essentially bilateral character of the system.'[18] When in June 1950 the books were closed on this scheme, $128.5 million of drawing rights, more than fifteen per cent of the total, remained unused.

Table 3 shows how imperfectly the Little Marshall Plan accommodated net surpluses and deficits. It financed 97 per cent of Austria's net deficits but only fifty-four per cent of Norway's and ten per cent of Portugal's. Drawing rights granted by Britain were a multiple of her net surpluses. Germany, a deficit country, granted drawing rights to other countries, while France received two-thirds of all the drawing rights granted despite being in surplus in intra-European trade.

Problems such as these did not provoke a crisis so long as American aid continued to flow. By the close of 1949, however, the end of the Marshall Plan was in sight. Hence, discussions were initiated that culminated in the European Payments Union.

The advent of the EPU

The EPU was designed as a two-year transitional arrangement,

Table 3 Drawing rights granted and used and their impact on net positions, October 1948–June 1950 (in millions of US dollars)

	Drawing Rights Granted[a]		Drawing Rights Received[a]		Net Surpluses or Deficits		
	Established	Used	Established	Used	Before drawing rights	After drawing rights	Net impact of drawing rights
I Belgium	618	494	11	9	526	40	−486
U.K.	488	382	122	62	27	−293	−320
Germany	238	216	187	118	−69	−166	−97
Italy	78	82[b]	27	–	305	224	−82
Sweden	86	85	10	8	149	72	−72
Switzerland	–	–	–	–	108	108	–
Net Grantors	1,508	1,258	356	197	–	–	−1,061
II France	51	58[b]	446	358	43	344	300
Greece	–	–	210	204	−232	−28	204
Netherlands	31	32[b]	226	226	−262	−67	195
Austria	6	4	157	157	−158	−5	153
Norway	24	11	135	134	−226	−104	123
Turkey	43	34	88	85	−79	−28	51
Denmark	12	9	36	35	−28	−3	26
Portugal	1	8[b]	21	18	−104	−94	10
Net Beneficiaries	166	155	1,318	1,216	–	–	1,061

Notes:

[a] Including a special credit line of $87.5 million granted by Belgium to the Netherlands ($38 million), the United Kingdom ($28 million), and France ($21.5 million), of which $39.1 million were actually used by the Netherlands ($38 million) and the United Kingdom ($1.1 million); but excluding minor readjustments.

[b] The use of multilateral drawings rights led, in a few cases, to drawings in excess of the drawing rights established by the grantor country.

Source: Triffin (1957), p.154.

at the end of which current account convertibility would be established. In structure it was a straightforward extension of the experiments in multilateral clearing that had been attempted since 1947. Under those arrangements, each participating country continued to make payments for imports using its own currency, and bilateral balances were accumulated at its trading partners' central banks. Under the EPU, in contrast, each country's net balances with each other country were reported at the end of the month to the Bank for International Settlements (BIS), the EPU's financial agent, which cancelled offsetting claims. Remaining balances were consolidated, leaving each country with liabilities or claims not on other countries but on the union as a whole. From the perspective of any one country's assets and liabilities in foreign currencies, it thus made no difference with which other European country or in what European currency trade was conducted. Only the overall balance of debits and credits in European currencies mattered at the end of the day.

Net debts could be financed initially with credits, but as they grew these liabilities had to be settled in dollars and gold. Each country received a quota equal to fifteen per cent of its total trade with the EPU area in 1949.[19] So long as its liability to the EPU remained less than 20 per cent of its quota, it could be financed entirely by credit. The net position was carried on the books of the EPU without requiring any payment. After the liability reached twenty per cent of the quota, settlement had to be twenty per cent in gold. Debts in the amount of forty, sixty and eighty per cent of quota required settlement in forty, sixty and eighty per cent gold.[20] (Here, as in the remainder of this discussion, settlement in gold is shorthand for settlement in gold or dollars.) Once the quota was exceeded, settlements with the union had to be entirely in gold. Not only was trade multilateralized, but its volume was stimulated by EPU credit lines.[21] Cumulative surplus positions were settled in similar fashion, although the proportions of gold payments escalated at a different rate (see Table 4).

Table 4 Initial schedule of settlements in the EPU (% of current deficit or surplus)

Cumulative surplus or deficit (% of EPU quota)	Country with cumulative deficit		Country with cumulative surplus	
	Gold	Credit	Gold	Credit
From 0 to 20	0	100	0	100
From 20 to 40	20	80	50	50
From 40 to 60	40	60	50	50
From 60 to 80	60	40	50	50
From 80 to 100	80	20	50	50
Overall	40	60	40	60

Source: Kenen (1991), p.256.

For debtor countries extended loans and being relieved of the need to settle bilaterally, the attraction of this system was obvious. But what was the attraction to creditors like Belgium and (after 1950) Germany in persistent surplus with the union? Accumulated claims could be converted into commodities or hard currency only partially and with delay. Until its quota was exceeded, a surplus country would receive gold amounting to only 40 per cent of its cumulative net exports to other EPU countries. Even when its cumulative surpluses exceeded its quota, rather than receiving payment in gold it might be asked to extend still more credit.[22] Unlike the rules governing excess deficits, the EPU Agreement said nothing about the settlement of excess surpluses.[23] All this represented a considerable potential cost to prospective creditors. Some, led by Belgium, pressed instead for an immediate transition to current account convertibility.[24]

What then induced them to participate? The answer comes in three parts. First, so long as surpluses and deficits remained relatively small, a larger proportion of gold payments was extended to creditors than was required of debtors. Once a fifth of each quota was utilized, debtors were able to settle with eighty per cent credit, but creditors received settlement half in convertible currency. This limited, though it did not eliminate, the costs mentioned above. Giving surplus countries more gold than was contributed by countries in deficit required working capital, however; this the US contributed in the form of a grant of $350 million of Marshall aid to the EPU.[25]

More importantly, membership came with conditions minimizing the scope for exploitation of creditors by debtors. When a member threatened to exhaust its quota, the EPU Managing Board comprised of independent financial experts reporting to the Council of the OEEC met to advise it and recommend corrective policies. Often discussions were initiated well before the quota was fully utilized, and it was made clear that the provision of exceptional assistance was contingent on the country's early adoption of policies of adjustment. Prospective creditors like Belgium had reason to hope that the debtors would adjust.

Most importantly of all, EPU membership required its participants to liberalize trade restrictions. Countries when joining pledged to eliminate discrimination against other participants based on balance-of-payments considerations. A Code of Liberalization formalized this commitment. By February 1951, less than a year after the EPU went into effect, all existing trade measures were to be applied equally to imports from all member countries.[26] Participants were required to reduce trade barriers by a given percentage of their pre-existing level, initially one half and then escalating to sixty and seventy-five per cent. The most internationally competitive European countries, such as Belgium, stood to gain disproportionately from such liberalization.

This link between the payments mechanism and intra-European trade liberalization, I shall argue in Chapter 5, was a key to the importance of the EPU. The intra-European trade liberalization made possible by the EPU in turn played a critical role in initiating the postwar era of rapid growth.

The growth of trade

The slow recovery of intra-European trade in the first post-war years is apparent in Table 5. The volume of Europe's exports to other continents had already surpassed 1938 levels by the second quarter of 1948; intra-European trade, in contrast, remained little more than two-thirds of pre-war levels. Exports to other European countries, as a share of total European exports, had been sixty-three per cent in 1938; by 1947 they had fallen to only fifty-five per cent. The comparable figures on the import side were fifty-five and thirty-seven per cent.[27] Only in the final quarter of 1949 was a significant expansion of intra-European trade evident, reflecting the rebound in business activity in the United States starting in the third quarter and (as demonstrated in Chapter 3) the effects of currency devaluation.

During the EPU years, intra-European trade expanded vigorously, from $10 billion in 1950 to $23 billion in 1959. Imports from North America grew more slowly, from $4 billion to $6 billion. Both intra-European trade and trade with the rest of the world expanded more quickly than European production, as Figure 1 makes clear. The spurt in European trade occurring in 1950–51 is coincident with the

Table 5 Quarterly movements in the value, volume and unit value of international trade (Billions of dollars in f.o.b. prices and index numbers)

	Intra-European Trade	Europe's Overseas Trade		United States		Rest of World		Total World Trade
		Imports	Exports	Imports	Exports	Imports	Exports	
Value								
1938 (quarterly averages)	1.7	1.4	0.9	0.5	0.8	2.1	2.3	5.7
1948 January–March	2.4	3.6	1.8	1.8	3.3	5.2	5.5	13.0
April–June	2.9	3.8	2.1	1.7	3.2	5.6	5.8	14.0
July–September	2.9	3.5	2.2	1.7	2.9	5.5	5.6	13.6
October–December	3.3	3.4	2.5	1.9	3.1	6.3	6.0	14.9
1949 January–March	3.3	3.6	2.5	1.8	3.3	6.1	5.7	14.8
April–June	3.5	3.8	2.4	1.6	3.3	6.0	5.7	14.9
July–September	3.4	3.3	2.3	1.5	2.7	5.6	5.4	13.8
October–December	3.3	2.8	2.0	1.8	2.6	5.3	5.3	13.2
Volume (Index numbers–1938 = 100)								
1948 January–March	60	113	88	152	204	103	92	97
April–June	71	117	101	141	201	112	96	103
July–September	72	108	104	145	183	104	89	99
October–December	82	98	120	155	200	129	96	110
1949 January–March	79	107	120	147	215	125	91	109
April–June	86	112	114	140	224	123	91	111
July–September	84	108	111	135	185	114	92	105
October–December	102	98	119	158	185	–	–	117

Source: United Nations, Economic Commission for Europe (1950).

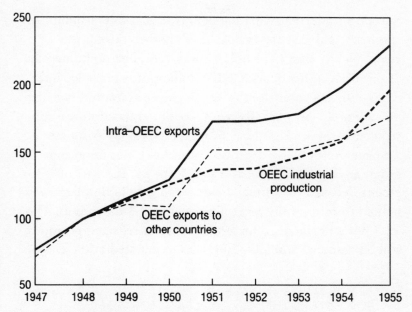

Figure 1 OEEC production and trade, 1947–55.
Note: 1948=100
Source: *OEEC Foreign Trade Bulletin* (various issues)

inauguration of the EPU. All this suggests that the liberalizing effect of the EPU was considerable.

Notwithstanding the relatively slow expansion of trade with the United States, Europe's dollar balance strengthened. Its hard-currency reserves doubled between the end of 1949 and mid-1956. The terms of EPU settlements were hardened (the agreement was revised to require debtors to pay and entitle creditors to receive higher ratios of hard currency to credit), and the removal of quantitative controls on intra-European trade was extended to Europe's trade with the dollar area.[28]

How important were multilateral cancellation of bilateral balances and swing credits, respectively, to the growth of

Europe's trade? Participating countries had $46.4 billion of surpluses and deficits against one another during the EPU years. Nearly half ($20 billion) was cancelled multilaterally (Table 6). Another quarter ($12.6 billion) was cancelled inter-temporally, as countries ran deficits in one month, financing them wholly or partially with credit, and surpluses subsequently, offsetting their previous position. Multilateral settlement, in other words, was nearly twice as important as swing credits (although, as Table 7 shows, the role of EPU credits declined over time). Payment in gold and dollars was limited to most of the remaining quarter ($10.7 billion). The $2.7 billion balance to be settled in credit reflected positions still outstanding when the EPU was terminated at the end of 1958.

Table 6   EPU settlements, 1950–58
(In billions of US dollars)

	Amount
Compensations	
Multilateral	20.0
Through time	12.6
Special settlements and adjustments	0.4
Balance settled in gold and dollars	10.7
Balance settled in credit	2.7
Balance to be settled	13.4
Total bilateral positions (deficits plus surpluses)	46.4

Source: Kaplan and Schleiminger (1989, Table 10).

In what sense was the EPU responsible for the expansion of trade depicted in Figure 1? While the surge in intra-European trade was concentrated in 1950–51, coincident with the inauguration of the EPU, much of that trade expansion reflected the experience of a single country: Germany. Other

Table 7 EPU settlements, July 1950–June 1956

	Total 1950–56	1950–51	1951–52	1952–53	1953–54	1954–55	1955–56
I In % of bilateral monthly balances							
A Compensations	75	66	74	92	70	86	64
1 Multilateral	46	49	40	55	48	47	37
2. Over time	30	17	34	37	22	39	27
B. Net settlements	25	34	26	8	30	14	36
II In % of Net Settlements							
A Gold and dollars	66	21	51	46	110	121	108
B EPU credits	23	57	39	22	-12	-21	-8
1 Current settlements	44	57	52	22	38	51	22
2 Amortization	-21	–	-13	–	-50	-72	-30
C American aid	11	22	10	32	2	–	–

Source: Triffin (1957), p.202.

factors besides the EPU importantly affected German trade, notably monetary reform, price liberalization and the associated recovery of production. Some might contend that the 1950–51 boom in intra-European trade is better attributed to the German *Wirtschaftswunder* (economic miracle, or era of sustained high growth) than to the EPU.

However, it can be argued – as I do in Chapter 5 – that the *Wirtschaftswunder* could not have taken the form of an export-led growth boom in the absence of the EPU. Without the EPU to underscore other European countries' commitment to accepting German exports, German producers would not have restructured along export-oriented lines. Without the EPU and allied institutions to provide reassurance that Germany would use her newfound market power benignly, other countries would not have kept their part of the bargain. The surge in Germany's European trade, and to some extent the recovery of German industrial production itself, thus reflect the effects of the EPU.[29]

Balance-of-payments adjustment under EPU conditionality

The EPU is said to have facilitated the resolution of balance-of-payments problems. Its Board extended supplementary credits to countries that exhausted their EPU quotas, attached conditions to their provision, and monitored domestic policy adjustments. Officials of countries receiving exceptional credits were required to appear at the monthly meeting of the EPU Board for questioning and to submit monthly memoranda for the Board's review.

The first episode dealt with by the EPU Managing Board

was the German crisis. In the initial five months of the EPU's operation (July-November 1950), Germany exhausted its quota. Trade deficits were to be expected: post-war reconstruction implied higher levels of domestic investment than saving. (While this was true of most Western European countries, in Germany the investment associated with post-war reconstruction only got underway following monetary reform in 1948.) But German deficits were larger than anticipated. The inauguration of the EPU in June 1950 coincided with the outbreak of the Korean War, which worsened the terms of trade of countries like Germany that imported primary commodities. Simultaneously, credit restrictions that had been imposed in conjunction with the monetary reform were relaxed, and taxes were reduced. Germany suffered cuts in American aid. And the country's EPU quota, calibrated on the basis of its 1949 exports and imports, was quickly dwarfed by the rapid expansion of trade that followed once the effects of the monetary reform were felt.[30]

With Germany barren of gold and continuing to run substantial deficits, DM-denominated payments for imports were made in advance of due date, and outstanding debts were left uncollected, exacerbating the reserve drain. Neighboring countries like the Netherlands and Denmark dependent on the German export market feared that Germany would revert permanently to quantitative controls. This might provoke the adoption of similar measures by the Netherlands and Denmark and the implosion of intra-European trade.

The Managing Board therefore negotiated with Germany a $120 million credit, conditioned on the government's adoption of a program of financial and economic adjustment. Conditions included commitments to maintain the existing exchange rate, to abstain from any form of deficit financing, and to increase taxes.[31] Germany was permitted to reimpose certain quantitative trade controls, but on an explicitly temporary basis.

The government quickly complied with the conditions. Turnover taxes were increased. The structure of income and corporate taxes was modified so as to restrict domestic absorption. To limit the extension of credit to industry (which had been used largely for the accumulation of inventories), reserve requirements on most banks were increased by fifty to one hundred per cent. The discount rate was increased by fifty per cent over the objections of Chancellor Konrad Adenauer, who feared that this would slow reconstruction. That the measure would enhance the prospects for an EPU credit line strengthened the hand of his opposition. As a result of the discount rate increase and related measures, net credits to the economy grew only a quarter as fast in the first half of 1951 as in the second half of 1950.[32]

These measures, together with the renewed controls, had an immediate impact on the balance of payments. Within weeks deficit gave way to surplus.[33] The German position strengthened sufficiently that the special loan could be repaid by the end of May 1951. Germany shifted to perennial creditor status within the EPU. The success with which the crisis was dispatched, without resort to measures that would have reversed the free market policies of the economics minister, Ludwig Erhard, is said to have greatly enhanced the reputation of the minister and his program.[34]

The Netherlands then experienced a similar crisis, partly because of the restrictive measures adopted in Germany.[35] The EPU increased the Dutch quota, and the government introduced restrictive fiscal and monetary policies designed to reduce investment by twenty-five per cent and consumption by five per cent.[36] By the end of 1951, the Netherlands like Germany had become a persistent creditor within the EPU.

Implications

The EPU was immensely successful in surmounting the obstacles to international transactions that had characterized the period of bilateralism. Settlements among the participating countries were multilateralized. Quantitative restrictions on intra-European transactions were relaxed. Trade among the participating countries expanded vigorously.

The expansion of intra-European trade and the success with which cooperation between the Managing Board and the participating countries dispatched balance of payments problems together suggest that the EPU was 'a system that worked.'[37] But was it the only system that might have worked? And if not, was it inferior to the alternatives? Answering these questions requires an analysis of the impediments to implementing the other obvious option: current account convertibility. This analysis yields a surprising answer that in turn suggests a perspective through which the true role of the EPU can be understood.

Notes

1 Other explanations for Europe's 'structural' deficit *vis-à-vis* the United States were the poor harvests of 1946 and 1947, the disruption of trade between Eastern and Western Europe, and wartime devastation in Europe's overseas possession such as Malaya and the East Indies.

2 To provide an idea of magnitudes, in the last of these three years European GNP was roughly $55 billion.

3 For Europe's overall trade, the corresponding figures were 121 and 130 per cent. United Nations (1949), Tables 61–2, pp. 96–7.

4 Diebold (1952), p. 16.

5 For details see Blancpain (1962).

6 BIS (Bank of International Settlements) (1948), p. 143.

7 United Nations (1950), p. 98. See also Bean (1948) and Rees (1963) for similar explanations.

8 Bean (1948), p. 404. Trade resumed only after France agreed to settle in gold part of the debt which had accumulated over and above the agreed credit ceiling.

9 United Nations (1950), p. 78.

10 Williams (1949), p.434.

11 Triffin (1957), p. 148.

12 Over the life of the agreement (from November 1947 October 1948), only $5 million of 'first-category compensations' was offset. Rees (1963), p. 70. In general, countries with surpluses against other European nations in possession of relatively ample reserves hesitated to have them offset, in the hope that they ultimately might secure hard currency in compensation. Bean (1948), pp. 408-10.

13 Rees (1963), p. 171.

14 BIS (1948), p. 148.

15 Triffin (1957), pp. 148–9.

16 This provided the surplus countries within Europe reason to resist the initiative. BIS (1949), p. 202.

17 Triffin (1957), p. 153. See also Kaplan and Schleiminger (1989), p. 25.

18 Rees (1963), p. 82.

19 Switzerland requested a larger quota, which other countries granted since the Swiss were expected to remain in surplus. Another prospective surplus country, Belgium, insisted on a smaller quota to limit the amount of credit it might have to extend to the rest of the EPU area.

20 The effective size of some countries' quotas was increased by giving them initial credit balances rather than starting them off with a zero net position against the union. Thus, they could run through their initial credit balance in addition to twenty per cent of their quota before having to make any settlements in hard currency. Initial credit balances were allocated to Austria, Greece, Iceland, the Netherlands, Norway and Turkey. Analogously, three countries expected to be structural creditors against the union – Belgium, the UK and Sweden – were made initial net debtors and compensated with conditional aid from the United States. See EPU (1951), pp. 12–4.

21 Momentarily I show that the multilateralization of trade through the cancellation of offsetting balances was actually more important than the extension of credits.

22 For example, Belgium, Portugal and Italy all accumulated surpluses in

excess of their EPU quotas in 1951 yet received settlement only up to a prescribed limit, half in gold and half in credit.

23 In June 1954, a revision to the agreement instructed debtors and creditors to settle bilaterally any balances that had been outstanding for extended periods. EPU debtors were to pay off these liabilities through periodic instalment payments over periods averaging seven years. This amortization of outstanding debts was viewed as necessary for the eventual re-establishment of convertibility.

24 For details on the Belgian negotiating position, see Milward (1984), chapters 6 and 8.

25 This $350 million was only a portion of the $600 million (reduced to $500 million by the US Congress) of ECA funds to be provided to countries that excelled in 'the aggressive pursuit of a program of liberalized trade and payments.' Wexler (1983), pp. 169–70. In this sense the carrot provided by the US extended beyond the $350 million of working capital per se.

26 Diebold (1952), p. 172.

27 Milward (1984), p. 214.

28 The terms of EPU settlements were 'hardened' twice. In July 1954 schedules for cumulative surpluses and deficits were made symmetrical. A flat 50 per cent gold ratio was applied to all quotas. In August 1955 the uniform ratio was raised to 75 per cent.

29 In Chapter 6, I report some estimates of a gravity equation of the determinants of international trade. One result that emerges from this analysis is that the positive association between EPU membership and trade is evident even when Germany is omitted from the sample of countries considered, which supports the notion that more was going on than simply rapid growth of German trade flows.

30 US aid deliveries declined from $1.35 billion in financial year 1948/9 to $480 million in calendar year 1950. Kaplan and Schleiminger (1989), p. 101. Germany's quota would have been more than half as large again if this rapid expansion of its trade had been anticipated. *The Economist* (November 4, 1950), p. 684.

31 Kaplan and Schleiminger (1989), p. 107–108.

32 Triffin (1957), p. 181.

33 Berger and Ritschl (1933) argue that the turnaround was accomplished in a matter of weeks. This suggests that the most important effects operated through expectations rather than current relative prices.

34 Kaplan and Schleiminger (1989), p. 115; see also Berger and Ritschl (1993).

35 Diebold (1952, p. 133) asserts that intense import competition from Belgium and the sterling area probably played a larger role in the country's EPU deficit.
36 For a detailed analysis, see *Statist* (1951).
37 The phrase is from Kaplan and Schleiminger (1989), p. 342.

Chapter 3

Was the EPU really necessary?

The EPU was a response to the perception that the other policy option, current account convertibility, was not feasible. But was this really this case? This chapter provides a two-part analysis of objections to convertibility. The first part describes the nature of the reservations voiced by contemporary observers. The second part analyzes the validity of those reservations in light of subsequent experience.

Contemporary objections to convertibility

Contemporaries identified a host of potential obstacles to convertibility in the aftermath of World War II. Some derived from the experience with convertibility following the first world war, others from the perception that the structure and performance of markets had changed in ways that rendered convertibility problematic.

The Historical Legacy

Prevailing attitudes about the regulation of international economic transactions following World War II were profoundly shaped by memories of the troubled aftermath of the previous war. Rather than sheltering their economies from relative price adjustments and attempting to insulate them from trade imbalances through the creation of a payments union, governments after World War I had maintained the convertibility of their currencies, allowing them to depreciate sufficiently to balance the sum of their current and capital accounts. That experience with convertibility and floating exchange rates was regarded as unsatisfactory. The relative prices of national currencies had fluctuated widely. Exchange rates, many complained, had been vulnerable to destabilization by speculators and subject to self-perpetuating cycles of inflation and depreciation.[1] In Germany and other Central European countries these unstable tendencies had degenerated into hyperinflation. The lesson drawn was the imprudence of delegating exchange rate determination to the market in the turbulent aftermath of war. Hence the preference for a payments union over convertibility.

A problem with this explanation is that post-World War I convertibility had been of an entirely different sort. Currencies had been convertible for both current- and capital account transactions. The destabilizing speculation or 'hot money flows' of which interwar observers complained reflected capital account transactions, as investors moved money from country to country in anticipation of subsequent exchange-rate changes. No one following World War II proposed the rapid reinstitution of capital account convertibility (which in fact occurred in many European countries only toward the end of the 1980s).[2] Convertibility following World War II meant current account convertibility – freedom to change domestic currency into foreign exchange for transactions in goods and services and repatriation of foreign-investment earnings only. Since the problem following World War I had been with convertibility for capital account transactions, there is no reason to believe that this experience should have created an aversion to current account convertibility following the second world war.

Structural Rigidities

Convertibility was feasible only if competitiveness could be restored *vis-à-vis* the United States. Real wages had to be reduced to price European manufactures back into international markets. But the militancy of European trade unions and the increasingly structured character of labor markets had, according to contemporaries, robbed real wages of their flexibility. Currency depreciation might therefore fail to reduce the ratio of European to American costs. Higher import prices would be passed through into higher export prices, with no improvement in European competitiveness or in the continent's balance of payments *vis-à-vis* hard-currency markets.[3]

Even if Europe succeeded through currency depreciation and other policies in enhancing the competitiveness of its exports, the trade balance still might not improve.[4] European buyers would not shift their purchases from imported to domestic goods because imports were comprised of essential foodstuffs, fuels and capital goods, only imperfect substitutes for which were produced at home. The inelasticity of the demand for capital goods was a particular problem. Germany had been the dominant supplier of capital goods to Europe in earlier decades. Her initially slow recovery from the war translated into a substantial, inelastic excess demand for American capital goods, exacerbating Europe's problem of real overvaluation.[5]

Given the inelasticity of import demands, this argument ran, changes in market exchange rates would not succeed in compressing imports. Similarly, the superiority of US goods and the unparalleled productive capacity of US industry meant that a change in relative prices might not help European goods penetrate American markets. (Exceptions, like exports of Scotch whiskey from the UK, were inelastically supplied in the short run.) The implication was that the trade deficit had to be restrained through the use of non-price measures, namely a payments union that perpetuated discrimination against American goods.

These arguments are reminiscent of the 'elasticity pessimism' of the 1940s.[6] That, of course, is precisely the point. Even those who conceded that devaluation might augment the volume of exports or limit the volume of imports argued that it would do so only at the cost of a substantial deterioration in the terms of trade. If the decline in export prices relative to import prices was sufficiently pronounced, the value of exports might fail to rise relative to the value of imports even if volumes moved in the desired directions.[7]

Deepening this elasticity pessimism was the prevalence of bilateral trade agreements and quantitative controls. The price elasticity of exports facing any one nation depended on the number of other countries offering market access. The fewer the open markets, the smaller the response to devaluation. Governments consequently faced a coordination problem: it was not feasible for any one country to devalue and adopt convertibility on its own, but if all the relevant countries devalued, restored convertibility and opened their markets simultaneously, the strategy might prove viable.[8] Devaluation was difficult to coordinate internationally, as both 1931 and 1949 had shown. Unable to solve this problem cooperatively, it is said, cautious governments retreated to inconvertibility.

Alternatively, the decision to opt for a payments union is sometimes rationalized in terms of the inadequacy of international reserves. Europe's balance of payments was sure to experience substantial shocks in the course of reconstruction and with the widely-expected post-war recession in the United States, not to mention unanticipated disturbances, the most important of which turned out to be the Korean War. Such disturbances would provoke intolerable exchange rate fluctuations unless policy-makers intervened. Intervention to support the exchange rate required international reserves. But European countries had expended the bulk of their reserves during wartime in the effort to purchase foreign supplies. Remaining reserves had been run down prior to the initiation of the Marshall Plan. In this view (for example, Emminger 1951), Europe lacked resources sufficient to stabilize its exchange rates.

Any of these problems, by itself, could have posed a formidable obstacle to the quick restoration of convertibility. The question is whether such problems were as severe as some accounts would have it. Or were these considerations really no more than minor impediments to the early restoration of current account convertibility, in which case it becomes necessary to search elsewhere for an explanation for the advent of the EPU?

Assessing the Obstacles to Convertibility

In this section I demonstrate that the obstacles to convertibility emphasized in the literature were nonexistent or overcome at an early date. I show, in other words, that the obvious prerequisites for the restoration of current account convertibility were already met by most EPU countries by the early 1950s and only a few years later in the exceptional cases like the UK

Janos Kornai has identified four relevant preconditions for viable convertibility.[9] First, a realistic exchange rate consistent with balance of payments equilibrium. Second, sufficient foreign exchange reserves. Third, elimination of monetary overhangs to prevent domestic absorption from crowding out exports and spilling over into unsustainable balance of payments deficits. Fourth, adequate wage discipline. I consider these conditions in turn.

Was a Market-Clearing Exchange Rate Within Reach?
The question is whether moderate devaluations could have eliminated current account deficits. To analyze it I follow the approach taken by Eichengreen and Sachs (1985) to the study of the 1931 devaluations. I use regression analysis to relate changes in the balance of payments to changes in the exchange rate and to other determinants. Using data spanning the 1949 devaluations, I regress the change in various components and determinants of the external accounts on a constant and the change in the nominal exchange rate against the US dollar. I consider a panel of countries, using the cross-section variation to identify the exchange rate effect.[10] The magnitude of the 1949 devaluations varied across countries, as Table 8 shows; this is what makes the procedure feasible.[11]

The basic data source is OEEC (1957), which presents information for seventeen OEEC countries, the US and Canada.[12] I excluded Iceland because fluctuations in its production and trade were dominated by the behavior of herring rather than economic policy.

The discussion in Chapter 2 of the evolution of Europe's trade in 1950–51 emphasized the extraordinary expansion of German exports, reflecting not only exchange-rate changes but also the surge in production that took place in the wake of the monetary reform. Whereas OEEC exports (valued at constant prices, including factor income receipts) increased by

Table 8 Devaluations: September 18, 1949, to the end of 1949

	Devaluations in Relation to the US Dollar %
The Sterling area except Pakistan	30
European Countries:	
Austria	53
Greece	33
Denmark	
Finland	
Netherlands	30
Norway	
Sweden	
France	22
Germany	20
Belgium	13
Portugal	13
Italy	8
Other countries:	
Argentina	47
Egypt	30
Canada	9

Notes Austria introduced multiple rates in December 1949, so that the end-1949 rate is an average. The pre-devaluation rate for the French franc is taken as the mean of the basic and free official rates.

Source: Tew (1965), p.170.

twenty-seven per cent between 1949 and 1950, those of the Federal Republic more than doubled. Restrictions on the level of German production were relaxed in 1948, and the currency reform inaugurated a period of rapidly increasing output and trade. Owing to these unusual conditions, I included a dummy variable for Germany in all regressions.

The first four equations in Table 9 show the response of the volume of exports to devaluation. A coefficient of 0.45 suggests that a thirty per cent devaluation, like that of Britain, raised the volume of exports by 13.5 per cent (.45 * 30) between 1949 and 1950. The analogous figure for 1949–51 is 15.3 per cent.[13] The positive sign and significance of the constant confirms that other factors (like the post-1949 US recovery and the Korean War boom) and not just devaluation contributed to the expansion of exports. Comparison of the two equations suggests that most of the exchange rate effect was felt between 1949 and 1950.

A potential objection to these results is that factors other than devaluation did not impact the US and other countries symmetrically.[14] The recession experienced in the United States in the first half of 1949 might have done more to depress exports *to* the US than exports *from* it. The third and fourth equations therefore add a dummy variable for the US. While its sign is consistent with the hypothesis, the coefficient differs insignificantly from zero. Inclusion of this variable reduces the coefficient on the exchange rate from 0.45–0.51 to 0.41–0.48.[15]

The next set of equations undertakes this analysis for imports.[16] Devaluation has the effect of reducing import volumes, but the coefficient on the exchange rate differs significantly from zero at standard confidence levels only when 1949 is compared with 1951. In contrast to exports, fully half the import response was delayed to the second post-devaluation year. These results depart from conventional wisdom according to which devaluation had no effect on imports because of quantitative controls.[17] The point estimates for 1949–51 are only consistent with this view insofar as they suggest a smaller proportionate change in imports than exports due to devaluation. They imply a 9.0 to 9.2 per cent decline in real imports between 1949 and 1951 as a result of a thirty per cent devaluation.[18]

The next four equations examine devaluation's impact on

Table 9 Effects of 1949 devaluations

Dependent Variable	Years	Constant	Exchange rate	Germany	US	n	R^2
				Independent Variables			
Exports	1949–50	0.60 (4.47)	0.45 (4.26)	0.90 (7.65)	–	18	.83
Exports	1949–51	0.67 (3.44)	0.51 (3.27)	1.50 (9.42)	–	18	.86
Exports	1949–50	0.66 (4.92)	0.41 (3.96)	0.88 (7.87)	–0.18 (1.55)	18	.84
Exports	1949–51	0.71 (3.45)	0.48 (2.94)	1.49 (9.20)	–0.19 (0.74)	18	.87
Imports	1949–50	1.31 (10.24)	–0.15 (1.48)	0.28 (2.50)	–	18	.37
Imports	1949–51	1.59 (8.39)	–0.30 (2.01)	0.25 (1.01)	–	18	.37
Imports	1949–50	1.30 (9.47)	–0.15 (1.36)	0.28 (2.42)	0.01 (0.13)	18	.33
Imports	1949–51	1.62 (7.96)	–0.32 (2.01)	0.24 (1.53)	–0.08 (0.46)	18	.33
Terms of Trade	1949–50	1.21 (14.70)	–0.20 (3.03)	–0.12 (1.72)	–	18	.43
Terms of Trade	1949–51	1.32 (7.24)	–0.28 (1.96)	–0.15 (1.00)	–	18	.24
Terms of Trade	1949–50	1.24 (14.73)	–0.22 (3.30)	–0.13 (1.73)	–0.09 (1.25)	18	.49
Terms of Trade	1949–51	1.40 (7.51)	–0.33 (2.29)	–0.16 (1.12)	–0.02 (1.35)	18	.33
Unit Labor Costs	1948–50	1.26 (7.10)	–0.34 (2.76)	–0.17 (1.23)	–	13	.48
Unit Labor Costs	1948–51	1.36 (5.51)	–0.37 (2.11)	–0.28 (1.50)	–	13	.38
Capital inflows	1949–50	–1.18 (2.38)	1.07 (2.59)	–	–	15	.34
Capital inflows	1949–50	–1.44 (2.73)	1.27 (2.92)	–	0.31 (1.26)	15	.42
Capital inflows	1948–50	–2.35 (1.43)	1.93 (1.51)	–	–	15	.15
Capital inflows	1948–51	–1.72 (1.14)	1.46 (1.25)	–	–	15	.11
Industrial production	1948–50	0.72 (5.11)	0.36 (3.53)	0.64 (5.30)	–	15	.76
Industrial production	1948–51	0.71 (3.40)	0.44 (2.92)	0.84 (5.01)	–	15	.72

Note: t-statistics in parentheses. n denotes number of observations.
Source: see text.

the terms of trade (the relative price of exports and imports). Consistent with assertions found in the literature, devaluation is associated with a deterioration in the terms of trade. The point estimates of the coefficient on the exchange rate suggest that a thirty per cent devaluation led to a 8.4–9.9 per cent deterioration in the terms of trade.[19]

At the same time the change in the terms of trade increased the demand for devaluing countries' exports, it encouraged firms to expand the supply of exportable goods by reducing unit labor costs in the tradables sector. The next two equations relate the change in unit labor costs in dollars in industry to the change in the exchange rate.[20] Whether 1948 is compared with 1950 or 1951, the exchange-rate elasticity is about a third – a thirty per cent devaluation against the dollar, in other words, reduced real labor costs in dollar terms by roughly ten per cent. The impact on output is evident in the next two equations, where industrial production (a measure of the production of tradables) is shown to have been positively associated with the magnitude of devaluation.[21] According to these results, a thirty per cent devaluation raised industrial production by 10.8–13.2 per cent.

The next four equations examine the relationship of devaluation to capital flows. There are theoretical grounds for anticipating a positive relationship. Devaluation by raising prices will reduce the real value of financial wealth; while some of the shortfall can be made good through foreign assets obtained by increasing exports and reducing imports, the rest will be obtained through capital inflows.[22]

The change in capital inflows between 1949 and 1950 is shown in the first two of these equations to have been positively (and significantly) related to the magnitude of devaluation.[23] The unit elasticity in the first equation means that a thirty per cent devaluation led to an improvement in the capital account equal to thirty per cent of initial exports. This supports Jacques Polak's contention that 'outward capital movements played a considerable role in worsening Europe's position before the devaluations, and their subsequent reversal accounted for a large part of the increase in reserves which followed the devaluations.'[24]

Yet this change in the direction of capital movements may have been dominated by anticipations of devaluation in 1949, which provoked capital outflows during the first three quarters of the year. I therefore reanalyzed capital movements using 1948 rather than 1949 as the base. (T.W. Kent (1950) suggests that the effects of anticipated devaluation on capital flows was limited to 1949.) One can reject the null hypothesis that this elasticity is zero at standard confidence levels. When capital movements in 1948 and 1951 are compared (on the grounds that inflows in 1950 may reflect repatriated flight capital), this conclusion is reinforced. It would appear that devaluation was associated with a dramatic shift in the direction of capital flows, as Polak suggested, but that this effect mainly reflected capital flight associated with devaluation expectations and subsequent repatriation.

What do these results imply for the effectiveness of devaluation? The OEEC's trade deficit (inclusive of factor income receipts and payments) was 6 per cent of exports in 1949. Ignoring capital account effects and considering only the induced change in exports, imports and the terms of trade, a 30 per cent devaluation, like that actually adopted by Britain and the Scandinavian countries (Table 8), would have eliminated two-thirds of this gap.[25]

Tests for nonlinear effects fail to support their existence — in other words, there is no evidence that larger devaluations had smaller proportional effects. Hence devaluations only somewhat larger than those actually implemented would have sufficed to bring Europe's current account into balance.[26] In answer to the question posed at the top of this section, a market-clearing exchange rate was within reach.

These effects, while at odds with the expectations of commentators writing before the fact (viz. Balogh 1949a, Kindleberger 1950), are consistent with analyses penned in the wake of the devaluations. As Kent wrote in 1950,

> Since devaluation the flow of dollar trade and payments has changed more sharply than was generally expected, while internally the economies of the devaluing countries have changed less than most people expected. At home, everything has gone on much as it was. Prices and wage-rates have both been sticky; employment has remained very high or even risen; there has been neither any large increase in inflationary pressure nor any serious retrenchment.[27]

Similarly, United Nations experts noted that European countries which devalued by twenty per cent or more increased their share of world markets by ten to fifteen per cent, while Western European countries which did not devalue – Belgium, Luxembourg, Italy and Switzerland – lost market share in virtually every commodity group. 'It must be concluded,' they wrote, 'that devaluation contributed to the improvement in the balance of payments on current account of the devaluing countries. . .'[28]

Four objections should be noted to the conclusion that a market-clearing exchange rate was within reach. One is that the improved external balance available to any one European country which devalued was not available to the group as a whole. Competitive devaluation, in other words, would have robbed exchange-rate changes of their effectiveness. But not all countries would have devalued in any case; importantly, competitiveness gains against the US would have remained. Furthermore, Table 9 is derived using a data set comprised of precisely such a set of simultaneous devaluations; the elasticities reported there, in other words, are already biased downward in a way that takes this account into effect. Finally, even if all countries had devalued simultaneously, trade balances still could have improved insofar as devaluation raised the relative price of traded goods and shifted resources into the production of tradables, making more output available for export. The final two equations in Table 9, documenting a positive effect of devaluation on industrial production (a crude proxy for tradables) confirm the operation of this effect.

A second potential objection concerns the appropriateness of considering current account balance rather than the overall balance of payments, including capital flows. Even if somewhat larger devaluations succeeded in restoring current account balance, this might not have sufficed for convertibility if capital accounts were in deficit. In fact, however, European countries in the early 1950s were capital scarce. Savings rates had not yet recovered to normal post-war levels, while the return on investment was exceptionally high during the recovery period.[29] Given convertibility, capital would have been more likely to flow in than out (although the results in Chapter 6 suggest that the magnitudes would have not been great). Insofar as capital flowed in, current account deficits could have been financed. The requisite devaluations would have been smaller, which reinforces the conclusion of this section.

A third potential objection is that countries would have supported their convertible currencies through the imposition or retention of trade restrictions.[30] Efforts to get them to adhere to a pre-established schedule for reducing trade restrictions would have been frustrated. This specter was raised, for example, in conjunction with discussions of whether to float the pound and restore its convertibility in 1952–53.[31] The present findings regarding the effectiveness of devaluation in fact cast doubt on these fears. Warnings of balance of payments difficulties leading to 'severe trade frictions' may have been warranted at the exchange rates prevailing prior to devaluation but not subsequently. If exchange-rate changes had been undertaken, there would have been no need to restrict trade.

A final potential objection is that the EPU was a response not to a balance of payments problem but to a dollar problem. European countries were in deficit against the United States in particular. Even if they had devalued by an additional ten per cent, many of them would have remained in deficit against the US, which was incompatible with the restoration of convertibility.

This point is germane only if most European countries did not restore convertibility simultaneously. If one such country devalued and restored convertibility but the others did not, it might find itself running surpluses against the rest of Europe and deficits against the United States; it might be unable to settle the latter in hard currency because it was earning only inconvertible claims through the former. But if all countries restored convertibility simultaneously, it would not matter from which ones they earned convertible assets and to which ones they incurred convertible liabilities. By definition, the dollar problem would have been eliminated along with the balance of payments problem.

Thus, while this objection does not overturn the conclusion that convertibility was viable, it points up a qualification. The restoration of convertibility in the early 1950s involved a coordination problem. What may have been possible for European countries as a group was not possible for any one. The coordination problem did not arise from the possibility, discussed above, that quantitative restrictions and inconvertible currencies rendered trade flows unresponsive to exchange-rate changes, therefore requiring all European countries to adopt convertibility simultaneously if they were to succeed in using exchange-rate adjustments to balance their external accounts. In fact, the cross-section regressions, estimated on data for the period of inconvertibility, show that trade flows were very responsive to exchange-rate changes even under these circumstances. Rather, the coordination problem arose because some countries, had they opted unilaterally for convertibility, might have had balanced trade overall but still run surpluses against inconvertible-currency countries and deficits against the hard-currency world. Only if the countries against which they ran surpluses simultaneously moved to convertibility would they be able to settle. Hence, convertibility required cooperation. European countries possessed a mechanism (the OEEC) through which information could be shared and the appropriate adjustments coordinated, but part of the problem still could have been that of synchronizing the transition to convertibility at an early date.

The Adequacy of International Reserves
One rebuttal to this conclusion concerning the viability of convertibility is that temporary shocks to the balance of payments to which countries wished to avoid having to adjust through a costly sequence of exchange-rate changes could not be financed given Europe's inadequate level of international reserves; countries would instead slow the pace of trade liberalization. As Margaret Hall put the point for Britain, 'It is

difficult to exaggerate the degree to which absolute smallness of the UK reserves of gold and dollars in the post-war period, by giving no margin wherewith to sustain short period dislocations . . . had contributed to the weakness of sterling in the postwar period.'[32] European observers continued to make the argument as late as 1954.[33]

In fact, for 1950 and later years, evidence of a reserve shortage is weak. For the industrial countries as a whole, the level of reserves was higher, relative to national income or the value of exports, than during the last period of convertibility: the interwar gold standard years 1926–29.[34] (See Table 10. The sample of countries is the same as that underlying the analysis of the effects of devaluation: all OEEC members plus the US and Canada.) Expressing all magnitudes in dollars, the ratio of gold plus foreign exchange reserves to GNP, which averaged 5.6 per cent in 1926–29, was to 8.1 per cent in 1950 and 6.9 per cent in 1951.[35] Trade having risen less dramatically than income, the point is reinforced when reserve-to-trade ratios are compared. Reserves as a share of exports averaged forty-four per cent in 1926–29 but reached fully 108 per cent in 1950, before declining to seventy-seven per cent in 1951 as trade recovered.

Since these aggregates fail to take into account the redistribution of reserves from Europe to the United States, I also calculated them for EPU members alone. The results, though less definitive, still fail to point to a shortage of reserves. The reserve-to-GNP ratio, having averaged eight per cent between 1926 and 1929, was only 6.7 per cent in 1950, and fell to a trough of 5.4 per cent in 1952 before recovering to about 7 per cent in 1954–55. Relative to the national incomes which European countries sought to smooth, then, EPU members were forced to make do with reserves about one-sixth

Table 10 International reserves as a share of exports and GNP,
1926–29 and 1950–55

| | Share of GNP | | Share of Exports | |
	All Countries	EPU Countries	All Countries	EPU Countries
1926	5.1	6.4	44.5	29.5
1927	5.5	5.8	40.6	29.2
1928	6.1	9.9	45.0	40.4
1929	5.9	9.8	45.8	39.7
1950	8.1	6.7	108.2	47.7
1951	6.9	5.6	77.1	33.9
1952	6.6	5.4	78.0	36.4
1953	6.5	6.4	79.5	45.4
1954	6.6	7.0	76.1	44.3
1955	6.2	6.9	75.1	46.0

Source: see text.

below customary levels. The picture is different when reserves
are compared to exports, however. The reserve-to-export
ratio, having averaged thirty-five per cent in 1926–29, was
fully forty-seven per cent in 1950, before falling back to a
post-war low of thirty-four per cent in 1951. Relative to the
trade that had to be financed, it is not obvious, then, that the
EPU countries possessed inadequate reserves.

This is not to deny that individual countries had meager
reserves. This was true of Austria and Germany, most of
whose reserves had been garnished or otherwise depleted. The
early restoration of convertibility by these countries would
have required special measures, such as quota drawings on the
IMF (International Monetary Fund) in the event of adverse
balance of payments shocks.[36]

Elimination of Monetary Overhangs
Kornai's third condition for viable convertibility is the elimination of monetary overhangs. If the pre-convertibility situation is characterized by price controls and an excess supply of

monetary assets, once convertibility is restored that excess liquidity, which has as its counterpart an excess demand for goods, will spill over into merchandise imports. Households and firms will use unwanted financial assets to import goods in short supply domestically. This will cause the exchange rate to depreciate or, if the authorities attempt to peg it, to a loss of reserves. If the monetary overhang is sufficiently large, reserves may be exhausted.

Price controls, a necessary condition for monetary over-hangs, remained in place over much of Europe in 1950, notably in the UK, Denmark, Sweden, Norway and the Netherlands.[37] Less certain is whether the excess monetary balances with which countries emerged from World War II had been eliminated. Some countries (Germany, Austria) undertook monetary reforms in the late 1940s, converting existing currency into new units at rates which mopped up excess liquidity.[38] Others (Belgium, Denmark, the Nether-lands) blocked money balances temporarily, giving industrial production (and money demand) time to recover, and converted a portion of such funds into forced loans. In still others (France, Italy) inflation reduced the real supply of money balances at the same time economic growth augmented the demand.[39] The question is whether the process had gone far enough by the early 1950s to eliminate monetary overhangs.

To gauge whether the supply of real balances had been reduced to levels compatible with convertibility, I employed the following procedure. For each of the major EPU countries, I estimated money demand functions for the period *after* convertibility was restored.[40] By definition, the level of money balances – or, more precisely, the relationship between money supply and the determinants of money demand – was con-sistent with the maintenance of convertibility in this period. I then used the estimated coefficients for the post-convertibility period, in conjunction with the actual values of the independent variables in the pre-convertibility years, to construct counterfactual forecasts of the level of real money balances that would have had to prevail during the EPU years had convertibility been restored. If actual money supply significantly exceeds simulated values prior to 1958, I conclude that there existed a monetary overhang that would have provoked current account deficits and reserve losses under convertibility.[41]

Using quarterly data from the beginning of 1959 through the end of 1967 (a period roughly matching the lifespan of the EPU), I regressed real money balances on a constant, output and an interest rate.[42] I then constructed counterfactual values for 1950I–1958IV (two pre-EPU quarters and the lifespan of the EPU).

The countries fall into three groups. In the first group, actual money balances differed by no more than two standard errors from the simulated values based on post-convertibility behavior. This is true of Belgium, France, Germany, Norway, Sweden and Denmark.[43] For these countries, then, monetary overhangs had been eliminated before the EPU commenced.

In the second group, actual money balances significantly exceeded forecast values at the beginning of 1950, but the discrepancy had been eliminated by the time the EPU came into operation in the second half of the year. This is true of Austria, the Netherlands and Italy.[44] In the first two cases, a decline in the level of real balances combined with growth in money demand (reflecting mainly rising levels of industrial production) to eliminate the overhang. In Italy, where a discrepancy existed only in the first quarter of the year, money supply continued to grow in the second quarter but slower than money demand. For these countries, then, monetary overhangs had existed prior to the EPU but were eliminated by the time it came into operation.

In the third group of countries – the UK and Ireland – the results indicate significant monetary overhangs. Simulated and actual real balances for these two countries are shown in Figure 2, along with two-standard-error bounds for the simulated values.[45] In Ireland, real money balances remain above forecast values until early 1952 or 1953, depending on the interest rate used in estimation and simulation.[46] In the UK, real balances significantly exceed forecast levels until about 1955. In the latter case, the delayed elimination of the discrepancy between actual and forecast money demands supports the notion that the most important elements of sterling convertibility had been restored *de facto* by 1955 or 1956. Before then but not after, controls on the freedom of residents and overseas holders of sterling to use them to finance imports from outside the sterling area resulted in an overhang of sterling balances inconsistent with the restoration of convertibility at the current exchange rate.[47]

To what extent would the exchange rate have had to be depreciated and prices been allowed to rise to eliminate these discrepancies between actual and simulated real balances? Except in the UK and Ireland, the differentials are small and could have been eliminated by the additional devaluations needed in any case to restore competitiveness *vis-à-vis* non-European producers. In the UK and Ireland, however, actual money balances initially exceed simulated values by fifty per cent. Devaluations of such magnitude, which raised the price level proportionately, would have been resisted by domestic electorates and foreign trade partners on the heels of the thirty per cent devaluations of 1949. In Ireland, by 1952 economic

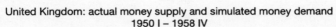

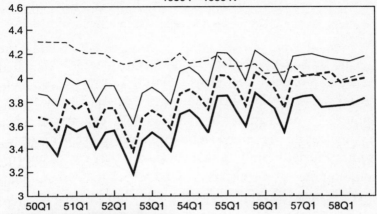

Dependent variable is log real money balances.
Interest rate is average rate for three–month Treasury Bills .

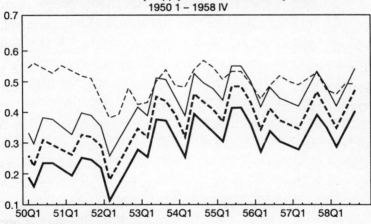

Dependent variable is log of real money balances.
Interest rate is official discount rate.

- - - - fitted   - - - - - actual   ———— upper band   ———— lower band

Figure 2   Actual and predicted money balances (in logs): UK and Ireland.

growth had eliminated much of the discrepancy, rendering relatively small exchange rate and price adjustments sufficient. In the UK, the problem persisted longer, until 1954 or 1955.

That Ireland and the UK emerge as the two countries with persistent monetary overhangs is hardly surprising. In 1950 Ireland was the only EPU country other than Turkey to be granted a derogation by the OEEC concerning the requirement that it remove quotas on seventy-five per cent of its intra-European trade, a step whose necessity can be understood in terms of the excess demand associated with a monetary overhang.[48] In 1948 the IMF, in analyzing wealth and liquidity overhangs in Europe, placed special emphasis on the UK situation, concluding that the overhang amounted a quarter to a half of national income.[49] At the annual meetings of the IMF and World Bank in Mexico City in 1952, the research staff held a seminar at which it argued that the UK still had substantial excess money balances. The danger that the UK would immediately exhaust its EPU quota was the principal objection to the clearing union scheme voiced by potential creditor countries like Belgium.[50] In 1952, fully two years into the system's operation, the BIS singled out the UK as the only major European country in which the ratio of money to national income remained significantly above 1938 levels.[51] *The Statist*, in an article published in October 1953, pointed to Britain as the single EPU country for which the removal of exchange controls remained problematic.[52] Colin Clark, in an article that preceded the 1949 devaluation, calculated that the pound might be significantly overvalued at a rate as low as $2.80.[53] An extensive subsequent literature (for example Meade 1953, Day 1954) considered the special problems of sterling convertibility. The fact that the UK quickly emerged as the largest debtor within the EPU is also consistent with this conclusion (although the export boom enjoyed by the commodity producers of the outer sterling area during the Korean War initially masked this situation).

The conclusion of this section is that except in the UK and Ireland monetary overhangs had been eliminated by the time the EPU commenced. Only in Britain did a serious problem persist. Even there it was essentially eliminated by the middle of the EPU years.

Wage Discipline

Judged on Kornai's first three criteria, convertibility appears to have been viable at the beginning of the 1950s for every EPU country but the UK and Ireland. If there were grounds for the skepticism of European policy-makers, these must lay in inadequate wage discipline. The question is whether convertibility, once restored, could have been defended, and whether wage trends might have undermined the competitiveness of convertible-currency countries. Was there a tendency in some countries, in other words, for unit labor costs to rise at unsustainable rates?

Actual wage behavior in the 1950s, insofar as it speaks to this hypothesis, lends it no obvious support. One of the most remarkable features of the 1950s was in fact the stability of unit labor costs. Table 11 shows their evolution in US dollars from 1948 until current account convertibility was restored a decade later. Unit labor costs in the US rose by twenty per cent over the decade 1948–58. In no EPU country did unit labor costs in dollars rise as quickly. (Canada, a non-EPU country, is a prominent exception but, revealingly, it had a floating exchange rate over much of the period.) The two European countries with the largest increases in dollar-denominated unit labor costs, France and the UK, were the two with the most persistent payments problems.

The evidence in Table 11 is not sufficient to dismiss the possibility that there existed problems of cost competitiveness due to the level of wages in post-1947 Europe, nor is it intended to do so. Indeed, Table 2 above confirmed that many European countries entered the period with unit labor costs that, relative to pre-war norms, had risen very significantly compared to those prevailing in the United States. Table 11 merely shows that such problems as existed were not exacerbated by the subsequent evolution of relative labor costs. It suggests only that if convertibility had been restored in 1950 and the evolution of unit labor costs had remained unchanged, the stability of the exchange rate would not have been undermined by inadequate wage discipline.

Implications

Most of the obvious preconditions for the viability of current account convertibility appear to have been met when European countries opted instead for the European Payments Union in 1950. A market-clearing exchange rate was within reach. Reserves were not grossly inadequate. Except in the UK and Ireland, monetary overhangs had been eliminated. If wage behavior had remained unchanged, exchange-rate stability would not have been undermined by the evolution of labor costs.

The question then becomes whether the behavior of labor costs would in fact have remained unchanged if governments had devalued further and restored convertibility. There is reason to think that the answer is no, and that this was the real obstacle to the early restoration of convertibility. I take up this issue and the further questions it raises in Chapter 5.

Table 11 Unit labor cost indices in US dollars (1948 = 100)

	1948	1949	1950	1951	1952	1953
Austria	100	97.23	47.46	56.28	62.65	54.06
Belgium	100	96.68	88.47	91.92	94.31	93.81
Canada	100	96.30	100.59	118.66	132.81	135.02
Denmark	100	94.74	72.10	77.25	81.51	87.04
France	100	86.45	77.78	91.98	100.61	104.77
Germany	100	79.65	59.14	61.88	63.79	63.77
Ireland	100	NA	64.53	70.98	78.71	76.17
Italy	100	89.68	73.79	72.06	72.95	68.98
Netherlands	100	89.13	65.94	69.17	67.90	64.06
Norway	100	94.14	64.78	70.13	75.58	75.89
Sweden	100	91.34	68.79	80.85	96.03	97.26
United Kingdom	100	91.72	68.74	75.14	81.82	83.29
United States	100	102.67	97.80	105.50	107.06	110.77

	1954	1955	1956	1957	1958
Austria	48.69	47.30	49.42	48.69	51.02
Belgium	91.67	88.86	92.95	103.40	NA
Canada	134.98	126.72	128.52	139.44	137.59
Denmark	86.53	85.26	87.60	89.84	93.08
France	101.79	100.49	99.57	101.31	98.61
Germany	61.25	60.74	66.06	71.10	75.09
Ireland	76.16	76.68	81.38	83.37	89.02
Italy	72.44	63.98	65.37	65.15	63.85
Netherlands	67.49	66.47	66.34	72.04	72.15
Norway	75.29	75.54	78.19	79.27	82.86
Sweden	98.09	102.40	107.15	110.75	NA
United Kingdom	83.24	85.34	92.61	95.35	98.60
United States	113.31	108.49	113.53	117.41	120.00

Note: Unit labor costs defined as (exchange rate*Wage)/(IP/Employment).
Source: Exchange rates from OEEC (1957). All other data from United Nations *Statistical Bulletin* (various issues).

First, however, it is necessary to confront an obvious objection to the conclusion that the immediate obstacles to the resumption of current account convertibility had been removed by the early 1950s. This is the fact that the UK had attempted to restore sterling's convertibility in 1947, an initiative which proved an unmitigated failure. Is this historical episode an indication, in other words, that convertibility remained an unattainable goal?

Notes

1 The definitive statement of this view was provided by Nurkse (1944).
2 See Nurkse (1953). Virtually the only voices advocating capital as well as current account convertibility in the 1950s were those of a group of extreme *laissez-faire* German economists led by Röpke.
3 See for example Kindleberger (1950), Chapter 10.
4 Balogh (1949b), pp. 231–3; Kindleberger (1950), pp. 209–10.
5 See Schmieding (1992).
6 Hirschman (1949) is representative of contemporary elasticity pessimism. The famous critique of this view is Orcutt (1950).
7 See Tew (1991).
8 Smithies (1950) provides a statement of this view.
9 Kornai (1990). He also lists a fifth – hard budget constraints to prevent public enterprises from demanding unlimited quantities of foreign exchange – that is not really applicable to the post-World War II Western European situation. The Western European analog would have been balanced government budgets, a condition which broadly obtained in all EPU countries by the beginning of the 1950s.
10 In the Appendix, the cross-section results are confirmed by a more elaborate pooled time-series cross-section analysis.
11 I address the possibility of reverse causation – or simultaneity bias – in note 14 below.
12 In some regressions (such as those explaining unit labor costs), it was necessary to omit selected countries due to missing data. Additional data for the US and Canada were drawn from Urquhart and Buckley (1965) and US Department of Commerce (1976), respectively.
13 These elasticities are biased downward insofar as devaluation took place at the end of the third quarter of 1949; comparisons between 1948 and

1950–51 show even larger effects. Thus the exchange rate coefficient in the export equation (the one including also the dummy variable for Germany) for 1948–50 is 0.73 (with a t-statistic of 4.39), while for 1948–51 it is 0.86 (with a t-statistic of 3.61). These results are consistent with the conclusion of Kent (1950) that the largest share of the effects of devaluation were evident by the end of the first year.

14 Another possible objection is that the results are contaminated by simultaneity bias: that the correlation between devaluation and export growth reflects the influence running from slow export growth in the preceding period (and hence the scope for rapid export growth subsequently) to devaluation. In fact, however, the decision of by how much to devalue appears to have been governed by other factors. Countries like Britain, Belgium and the Netherlands whose exports had grown the most quickly in the immediate post World War II years were among those which undertook the largest devaluations. As a formal test for simultaneity, I used Hausman's procedure, instrumenting the current exchange rate with lagged export growth, without turning up evidence of significant simultaneity bias.

15 When 1948 is used as the base year, the respective coefficients are 0.68 (with a t–statistic of 3.92) and 0.82 (with a t-statistic of 3.21). Thus, these results are consistent with the conclusions of Kent (1950), who regards the impact of the US recession and recovery on European exports as secondary to the effects of devaluation.

16 Again, a Hausman test using lagged imports as an instrument failed to turn up evidence of significant simultaneity bias.

17 Harrod (1963), p. 127.

18 These effects fall to less than half their previous size when the longer periods starting in 1948 are considered.

19 The effect increases slightly in size when the analysis begins from a base of 1948. This is a context in which many readers may worry that the change in the dependent variable (here, the terms of trade) had other causes (different rates of inflation at home and abroad due to the Korean War, for example). It is reassuring therefore that the structural equations reported in the Appendix are consistent with the analysis in Table 9, and that a Hausman test using lagged terms of trade as in instrument failed to reject the null of no simultaneity bias.

20 The data are constructed using the methods and sources of Table 2, with one exception. In Table 2 all unit labor costs are expressed relative to the US, with 1938 equalling 100. Here unit labor costs in dollars are instead benchmarked to 100 in 1948 for each country.

21 1948 rather than 1949 is used as the base year to eliminate the distortionary effects of the 1949 US recession. The results are essentially the same when 1949 is used so long as a dummy variable for the US is included. Given the magnitude and significance of the dummy variable for Germany, I experimented with a dummy variable for Austria, another country which underwent currency devaluation and price liberalization at approximately the same time, and whose large devaluation and pronounced increase in industrial production could have been driving the results. But here, as in previous equations, the dummy variable for Austria was insignificant at standard confidence levels.

22 For a theoretical analysis of these relationships, see Dornbusch (1974).

23 The absolute change in capital flows between successive years is scaled by exports in the earlier year. Taking percentage differences as in the preceding equations for exports, imports and the terms of trade is not feasible because some capital flows are negative in the base year. Capital flows include errors and omissions on the grounds that these reflected mainly unrecorded capital movements. This measure is computed from figures provided by the same sources as for the export and import equations above.

24 Polak (1953), p. 2.

25 I use the average of the point estimates for 1949–50 and 1949–51 in these calculations. Both the export and import effects improve the trade balance, while the induced deterioration in the terms of trade worsens it, by an amount that roughly exactly offsets the import-side effect.

26 Note that I am discussing here Europe's overall current account position rather than the current accounts of individual European countries. Of course there is no reason why, after restoring convertibility, individual European countries could not have continued to run surpluses and deficits *vis à-vis* one another so long as these were transitional. Below (in the sections on monetary overhangs and international reserves), I discuss the problems of particular European countries.

27 Kent (1950), pp. 22–3.

28 United Nations (1951), pp. 104–5.

29 Relevant data are provided by Eichengreen and Uzan (1992).

30 'There is not the slightest reason to doubt,' wrote Thomas Balogh in 1949, 'that even a partial convertibility of European currencies into dollars would now cause a wholesale restriction on European trade . . .' Balogh (1949b), p. 87. For parallel warnings see United Nations (1948), p. 105.

31 See Kaplan and Schleiminger (1989), chapter 11.

32 Hall (1950), p. 868.

33 See for example *The Statist* (1954).

34 I consider only the 'heyday of the interwar gold standard' (1926–29), before deflation and the liquidation of foreign exchange reserves set in. For details on changes in reserve composition and levels after 1929, see Eichengreen (1990). In the present discussion I do not consider changes in external liabilities as well as in external assets. But in Chapter 4 I discuss in detail the evolution of external liabilities for the country where they were surely most important: the United Kingdom.

35 The movement between 1950 and 1951 reflects the rise in the denominator due to the Korean War inflation. The ratio falls slightly thereafter, to 5.5 per cent in 1952, 6.5 per cent in 1953, and 6.2 per cent in 1955. Data on reserves and exports for the interwar years are drawn from League of Nations sources, notably the *Monetary Review* (various issues) and the *Monthly Bulletin of Statistics* (various issues). Data on national income are taken from Mitchell (1976, 1983). For the 1950s all data are from OEEC (1957) and the IMF's *International Financial Statistics*.

36 Alternatively, it might have been possible for them to restore current account convertibility without resorting to the IMF by allowing the exchange rate to float. In principle, convertibility is possible irrespective of the level of reserves so long as countries allow the exchange rate to adjust to clear the market for foreign exchange. This, of course, was the point of Friedman (1953), as noted in Chapter 1. Although floating was not consistent with the IMF Articles of Agreement, this did not prevent important trading countries, notably Canada, from pursuing the option. See Dam (1982) for an analysis of the Fund's ambiguous stance on the issue.

37 For details, see United Nations (1950), p. 56, and BIS (1950), pp. 106–7. An excellent discussion of the implications for the balance of payments of these controls and the excess demand with which they were associated is Hawtrey (1953).

38 See Dornbusch and Wolf (1990). The reference to a successful Austrian monetary reform refers to the second such attempt in 1948.

39 For details, see Jacobsson (1950) and Casella and Eichengreen (1993).

40 For a few small countries, adequate data did not exist to implement this procedure. However, results are presented below for all of the major EPU members.

41 A central assumption is that the demand for money under convertibility,

which is not observed before 1959, was stable across the pre- and post-convertibility periods. (By 'not observed' I mean that prior to 1959 the money market was not necessarily in equilibrium: in some countries there may have existed an excess supply of money and an excess demand for goods that were supported by price controls and foreign exchange restrictions.)

42 Specifically I regressed real money balances (the IMF's narrow money measure deflated by the consumer price index) on a constant, a measure of the level of activity (industrial production) and an interest rate. Seasonal dummy variables were also included. The sample includes quarterly data from the beginning of 1959 to the end of 1967. For Italy, consistent interest rate data were not available for both the estimation and simulation periods, so money balances were regressed on output and a constant term alone. Data on money, prices and output are drawn from various issues of the IMF's *International Financial Statistics*. Ancillary interest rate data are taken from various issues of the OEEC's *Statistical Yearbook*.

43 Norwegian money balances also fall within two standard errors of forecasts, but there the limitations of pre-1955 data do not permit the construction of forecasts prior to that date. BIS (1952, p. 182) notes, however, that Norway was one of three Western European countries (along with the UK and Sweden) where the ratio of money to national income was significantly higher than in 1938. Actual values for Sweden prior to 1954–IV may be subject to error, because monetary aggregates were redefined at that point. I used overlapping observations for the new and old series in 1955I to rebenchmark the pre-1955 series.

44 In Austria, actual values creep up above the forecasts starting in 1953, but the adjustments needed to eliminate the discrepancy remain relatively small.

45 The simulated values display pronounced seasonal fluctuations. Since the estimated money demand functions for the post-1958 period *included* three quarterly dummy variables, the seasonality in the pre-1958 simulations therefore reflects a *change* in the seasonal pattern of the explanatory variables before and after the restoration of convertibility. In the case of Sweden, for example, industrial production has a much larger seasonal component before 1958 than after. An alternative approach is to deseasonalize industrial production separately for the pre- and post-convertibility periods, estimate money demand functions for the second period using the deseasonalized data, and simulate for the pre-convertibility period also using deseasonalized data. This produces a

smoother seasonal pattern of fitted values and standard error bounds but does not change the substantive implications of the analysis in any way.

46 The gap disappears by 1952 when the official discount rate is used, as in Figure 2, by early 1953 when the rate on long-term government bonds is used instead. Not much credibility should be invested in the small fluctuations evident in 1952 and 1953; for these two years quarterly money supply figures were not available, and annual averages (deflated by each quarter's consumer price index) are used instead.

47 That British policymakers, when contemplating convertibility in 1952, concluded that the pound would have to float downward in order to permit the maintenance of external balance is consistent with this finding. Note that the methodology necessarily elides the external (sterling balance) overhang and the internal (monetary) overhang. The limited availability of quarterly data on the former obstructs efforts to distinguish them systematically. In any case, the sum of the two over-hangs is likely to be relevant for the sustainability of convertibility.

48 Bossuat (1992), p. 733.

49 See Bernstein (1948).

50 Diebold (1952), pp. 64–9; Wexler (1983), pp. 166–7.

51 BIS (1952), p. 182 also mentions two smaller countries, Norway and Sweden, in this connection. Given the results for Ireland reported below, it is worth noting that the BIS provides no analysis for that country.

52 *Statist* (1953), p. 520.

53 See Colin Clark (1949), p. 206.

Chapter 4

Implications of the 1947 sterling crisis

The idea that many of the preconditions for convertibility obtained within five years of World War II runs up against a powerful counterexample: Britain's abortive restoration of convertibility in 1947 which had to be abandoned after barely a month. This episode entered the lore of post-war international finance as proof positive that convertibility was infeasible. In this chapter I show that the events of 1947 in fact fail to contradict the conclusion that the obvious requirements for convertibility were met in most countries by the early 1950s.

The American loan

In 1946, the United States extended a $3.7 billion loan to finance Britain's balance of payments requirements for three years. Officially the loan for was $4.1 billion, but $0.4 billion was for Lend–Lease goods already in the pipeline. It bore a two per cent rate of interest following a five year grace period and was to be amortized over fifty years. Annual instalments of principal and interest averaged $140 million at an actuarially equivalent interest rate of 1.6 per cent.

As a condition for furnishing these funds, the US required

the British government to restore current account convertibility. The precise requirement was for convertibility to be resumed within a year of the loan's approval by the American Congress. The Anglo–American agreement thus superseded the transitional period of inconvertibility, expected to last five years, that had been built into the Bretton Woods Agreement. US officials were particularly anxious to secure Britain's commitment to convertibility in light of its ties to the sterling area. The Bretton Woods Agreement had not completely eliminated their fear that Britain would use sterling's inconvertibility as a device to extend commercial preferences to the Commonwealth and Empire.

When sterling's convertibility was restored on schedule, on 15 July 1947, a massive hemorrhage of reserves ensued. Reserve losses in the single month of convertibility exceeded $1 billion. Adding losses over the period between approval of the loan and the resumption of convertibility, fully $3.6 billion of the $3.7 billion credit line was dissipated. A loan designed to last three years lasted just one.

This episode demonstrated clearly that sterling convertibility was not viable in 1947. But this disastrous episode reflected special problems, not all of which were shared by other countries and many of which Britain itself had resolved by the early 1950s. The events of 1947 therefore fail to overturn the conclusion that the obvious prerequisites for convertibility were met by most European countries when they opted instead for a payments union.

Theoretical perspectives

The massive drain of reserves following the restoration of sterling convertibility was a classic speculative crisis.

Anticipating that the authorities would be unable to maintain the convertibility of sterling at the rate of $4.02, those in a position to do so scrambled to convert their sterling into dollars before the opportunity was withdrawn. The closer the denouement, the more desperate the scramble. Quickly the situation degenerated into a full-fledged crisis.

Given the nature of the episode, it is illuminating to refer to the theoretical literature concerned with speculative attacks on fixed exchange rates (Krugman 1979; Flood and Garber 1984). The determinants of Britain's crisis turn out to be somewhat different than those highlighted in the theoretical literature. But this very fact helps to clarify the factors responsible for the events of 1947.

In standard models, the crisis reflects the incompatibility of underlying monetary and fiscal policies with the commitment to a pegged exchange rate. As typically formulated, that incompatibility results from the domestic government's practice of running persistent budget deficits which it finances by printing money.[1] Investors wishing to hold domestic and foreign assets in relatively stable proportions are unwilling to allocate an ever-growing share of their portfolios to domestic currency. As the authorities churn out money, investors attempt to swap a portion of it for foreign assets. This increase in the demand for foreign assets (equivalently, increase in supply of domestic assets) puts upward pressure on the domestic-currency price of foreign securities – that is, it creates pressure for exchange-rate depreciation. Since the authorities are committed to pegging the exchange rate at its current level, they purchase the excess supply of domestic assets for foreign securities in their possession – in other words, by using their international reserves. Investors realize that once those reserves are exhausted the authorities will have lost their ability to peg the exchange rate. Anticipating the inevitable, they scramble to reduce their holdings of domestic assets once reserves fall to a critical threshold. This is the speculative attack. When it occurs, the authorities' reserves are exhausted, forcing them to depreciate the exchange rate.

Empirical modifications

Strictly speaking, the standard model is not applicable to the events of 1947. For one thing, Britain's budgetary imbalance had already been corrected. The deficit of the combined public authorities was reduced by eighty per cent between 1945 and 1946 and extinguished in 1947.[2] Nor did excessive lending by the British banking system raise the rate of domestic credit creation to unsustainable heights. The UK money supply grew by only four per cent over the course of 1947, which seems insufficient to account for the crisis.[3]

It is still possible to understand the events of 1947 in terms of these theoretical models once it is understood that they require persistent money creation only because they assume continual portfolio balance. This assumption is not appropriate to 1947. Prior to the resumption of convertibility, investors were not in fact allowed to freely exchange domestic and foreign assets for one another or for merchandise. Rationing and price controls constrained them. Although per capita consumption had been reduced by about 16 per cent at the height of the war, real earnings rose steadily and by the termination of hostilities were considerably higher than in 1938.[4] The UK money supply tripled between 1938 and 1947, a period over which GNP at current prices rose by only eighty-six per cent, increasing the supply of domestic real balances by nearly two-thirds.

Meanwhile, private and official holdings of gold and dollars (US and Canadian) in the UK had fallen by fifty per cent.[5] Foreign assets had been requisitioned in support of the war effort, and controls on commodity exports and capital flows prevented investors from replenishing them. If the desired division of portfolios between domestic and foreign assets was the same in 1947 as in 1938, a very considerable suppressed demand existed to exchange domestic for foreign assets. Investors would have wished to convert £1 billion into foreign assets as soon as they had the opportunity.[6] And to the extent that controls and rationing had forced them to build up unwanted financial assets, the excess would – and did – spill out into a current account deficit.

Overseas residents were the subset of investors best positioned to circumvent restrictions limiting sterling convertibility to transactions on current account. This was what rendered the so-called 'sterling balances' (sterling in overseas hands) so important. Between 1939 and 1945 the Commonwealth and Empire had accepted sterling in payment for the raw materials used to fuel the war machine, which they were asked to hold rather than to spend on imports of their own. At the war's end, overseas sterling was more than £3.5 billion, or a third of UK GNP. Most of this was held by the countries of the sterling area. (See Table 12.) Overseas sterling swamped the UK's gold and dollar reserves of £0.6 billion at the end of 1946 and the £1.25 of hard currency provided by the American Loan agreement.[7] If merely half the outstanding sterling balances were converted, they would exhaust Britain's reserves and the credit line. And overseas sterling balances had risen by a factor of eight over the course of the war, implying a considerable unsatisfied desire to convert them into commodities and hard currency.

Table 12 Overseas sterling holdings 1945–58
(£ million)

1945	31st Dec. 1946	31st Dec. 1947	31st Dec. 1948	31st Dec. 1949	31st Dec. 1950	31st Dec. 1951	31st Dec. 1952	31st Dec. 1953	31st Dec. 1954	31st Dec. 1955	31st Dec. 1956	31st Dec. 1957	31st Dec. 1958
A Overseas sterling holdings													
Sterling area countries	2,397	2,367	2,250	2,155	2,158	2,549	2,636	2,542	2,798	2,924	2,879	2,856	2,700
Non-sterling countries													
Dollar Area	34	33	18	19	31	79	38	34	62	97	58	37	35
Other Western hemisphere countries	163	212	235	135	80	45	57	6	40	8	9	32	31
OEEC countries:													
EPU reported accounts }	351	363	419	309	356	90	122	60	45	35	34	24	35
Other						224	206	179	178	209	179	169	255
Other Non-sterling Countries	622	635	476	534	518	496	518	398	370	430	417	303	244
Total Non-sterling Countries	1,170	1,243	1,148	997	985	934	941	677	695	779	697	565	565
Total All Countries	3,567	3,610	3,398	3,152	3,143	3,483	3,577	3,219	3,493	3,703	3,576	3,421	3,265
Non-Territorial Organizations	–	26	388	398	576	577	566	567	511	476	469	669	645
Total	3,567	3,636	3,886	3,550	3,719	4,060	4,143	3,786	4,004	4,179	4,045	4,090	3,915
Total as a share of GNP	36.0	36.2	36.0	29.7	29.5	30.5	28.1	23.8	23.5	23.2	21.0	19.6	17.7
Total as a share of reserves	585	547	759	777	617	345	497	586	445	424	534	512	482
B Acceptances outstanding													
Sterling Area Countries }			30	53	50	71	92	70	69	102	101	126	9
Non-sterling }													138
Total			30	53	50	71	92	70	69	102	101	126	147
C UK credit(+) or debit(−)													
Balance in EPU					–	80	−166	−219	−198	−120	−121	−125	−136
D UK official holdings of non-dollar currencies													
OEEC Countries	7	39	35	38	23	51	14	37	8	10	9	10	32
Other Non-sterling Countries	1	2	2	–	–	–	–	3	2	3	4	4	4
Total	8	41	37	38	23	51	14	40	10	13	13	14	36

Sources: UK HM Treasury (1959, p.59), and Feinstein (1972, Appendix Table 3).

The authorities, aware of these problems, sought to limit convertibility to transactions on current account. Residents were not permitted to obtain dollars from the Bank of England except for authorized merchandise imports. Those without UK nationality were permitted to convert into dollars only those new sterling claims which they acquired by exporting goods and services to the UK, plus a limited amount of blocked sterling negotiated with Britain year to year. Starting in October 1946, the Government signed a series of agreements with the main non-sterling countries intended to limit dollar convertibility to currently-earned sterling. At least half of outstanding overseas sterling balances were officially blocked in this way.[8] Transfers into other currencies were subject to exchange control and required official sanction.

Possessing considerable leverage over the members of the sterling area, the UK government pressed them to refrain from running down their sterling balances. While their sterling was formally convertible, at least for certain specified transactions, their central banks cooperated with the UK in applying voluntary restrictions. The colonies had little choice: Ghana and Malaya, for example, which generated significant dollar receipts, were required to add these to the sterling area's common pool, much of which was used to buy UK imports.[9]

Powerful incentives existed to circumvent these restrictions. The British authorities could not monitor the net exports of goods and services to the UK of each country in each month. It delegated this responsibility to foreign governments, which had every incentive to overstate the extent to which their residents' sterling balances were newly acquired through current account transactions. Restrictions to prevent inconvertible sterling balances from being used to pay for imports were widely violated, releasing currently earned

sterling for exchange into dollars.[10] The UK's current account
deficit can account for little more than half of the loss of gold
and dollars in 1946 and 1947. The problem worsened with
time: the deterioration of the current account between 1946
and 1947 can explain only a fifth of the increase in the dollar
outflow in the latter year.[11] The rest reflected leakages under-
mining the British authorities' efforts to segregate current and
capital account transactions.[12]

As the crisis mounted and speculators began to anticipate
devaluation or a possible ban on British foreign investment in
the sterling area, capital took flight to South Africa and
Australia. The largest single flow was destined for South
Africa, where the discovery of gold in the Orange Free State
and associated construction and manufacturing booms
offered new investment opportunities. In addition, commercial credits to those without UK nationality were built up
through the operation of leads and lags. Thus, even in the
presence of restrictions on capital account convertibility
designed to limit currency speculation, there remained ample
scope to shift into foreign exchange in anticipation of the
inevitable devaluation.

Implications

Britain's inability to maintain sterling's convertibility in 1947
is no mystery. It reflected a disequilibrium in financial markets
providing powerful incentives to convert sterling into foreign
exchange. Investors used every device at their disposal to
circumvent the Government's effort to restrict convertibility
to current account transactions. The only puzzle is why British
and American authorities did not anticipate the problem.[13]

This analysis of the 1947 crisis suggests, at the same time, that many of the obstacles to sterling convertibility had been removed by the early 1950s.[14] While the monetary overhang had not been eliminated by the beginning of the decade, it had been greatly attenuated. As Ralph Hawtrey noted in 1953, British GNP had increased by sixty-five per cent over the preceding seven years, while the money supply had increased by only ten per cent.[15] The current account deficit, necessarily settled by expending reserves or augmenting overseas sterling balances, was eliminated by the early 1950s.[16] While there was no decline in the magnitude of the sterling balances, their growth was curtailed after 1947. Economic recovery and inflation combined to reduce them as a share of GNP. By the end of 1948, sterling balances had fallen to less than thirty per cent of national income, where they remained (Table 12). After 1951 their end-year value never exceeded twenty-four per cent of GNP.

Britain's overseas liabilities thus constituted less of a threat to convertibility after 1947, and especially after 1951, than before. Meanwhile, UK reserves rose from $1.3 billion in early September 1949 to $2.0 billion at the end of March 1950 and $2.4 billion at the end of June. Sterling balances, which had once been nearly eight times reserves, fell to 5 times and less. While the evidence of monetary overhang in Chapter 3 suggests that the problem had not been eliminated by 1950, it had been greatly reduced.

Thus, the special circumstances that had undermined Britain's effort to restore current account convertibility in 1947 – notably an excess supply of sterling balances in the hands of those overseas residents best positioned to convert them and a current account deficit continually augmenting those deficits and depleting Britain's remaining reserves – had been greatly attenuated by the early 1950s. Britain's inability to restore convertibility in 1947 fails to undermine the argument that the obvious preconditions for its maintenance were met in most countries by the early 1950s.

Notes

1 In this setting, the distinction between money and bonds is not important. When there is the possibility of a large devaluation within a short period, investors will resist holding both domestic currency and bonds. From this point of view it makes no difference whether the authorities rely on money or bond finance.

2 The current balance of the combined public authorities swung from a £1.8 billion deficit in 1945 to a £363 million deficit in 1946 and a £219 surplus in 1947, mainly through substantial cuts in expenditure on goods and services. Feinstein (1972), Table T36.

3 This is the growth rate of Capie and Webber's (1985) M3 between the end of successive years. Estimates presented by Triffin (1957, p. 318) suggest an even slower growth rate.

4 Cairncross (1985), pp. 11–12.

5 Data on money supply and GNP are taken from Triffin (1957), p. 320, those on gold and dollar holdings from ECA (Economic Cooperation Administration) (1951).

6 British residents had held £0.9 ($4.2) billion in gold and dollars plus £3.2 billion of domestic money (M3) at the end of 1938 (Capie and Webber 1985), so that domestic assets comprised eighty per cent of the total. To hold this same proportion in 1947, investors would have wished to exchange more than £1 billion of domestic M3 for dollars or gold. (Foreign assets had fallen to $2.1 (or £0.5) billion, whereas M3 had risen to £8.2 billion. Twenty per cent of the total portfolio of £8.7 billion was £1.64 billion, or more than £1 billion in excess of actual gold and foreign currency holdings.)

7 If total sterling area gold and dollar reserves are considered instead, these came to £664 million at the end of 1946. Balogh (1954), p. 496.

8 While accumulated balances could not be converted into dollars, so-called 'transferable account countries' could shift them freely throughout the transferable account area. Dow (1964), p. 23.

9 Armstrong, Glyn and Harrison (1991), p. 62.

10 Rees (1963), p. 60.

11 Dow (1964), p. 24.

12 For contemporary recognition of this fact, see Robbins (1947). The fact of capital account restrictions explains why British reserves drained away at a slow but steady rate without provoking a speculative attack which liquidated the gold and foreign exchange which remained.

13 Dow (1964, p. 23) suggests that the British authorities had hoped for cancellation of most of the sterling balances as war debts; in fact, only Australia and New Zealand accepted a partial cancellation.

14 This is also the conclusion of Haberler (1954) and Jacobsson (1954), pp.144–6.

15 Hawtrey (1953), p. 434.

16 The improvement in the current account reflected a rise in domestic savings rates rather than a decline in the investment share of GNP. Pent-up demands left over from wartime depressed savings in the immediate postwar years, but the effect was temporary. UK saving rose from eight per cent of GNP in 1947 to 13 per cent in 1948–51 and sixteen per cent in 1952–60. Savings rates are calculated as investment plus the current account balance as a share of GNP, as in Eichengreen and Uzan (1992). The improvement in the current account balance was achieved through the mechanisms described in Chapter 3, notably the improvement in cost competitiveness associated with the 1949 devaluation. A caveat is that the dollar deficit remained – that is, to some extent British credits were still in inconvertible currencies, while her debits were in gold and dollars. Still, while dollar area trade remained in deficit, the dollar balance improved faster than the current account balance with the sterling area. Balogh (1954), pp. 491–2.

Chapter 5

Why the EPU was adopted

That the obvious prerequisites for current account convertibility were satisfied by the early 1950s would seem to
make the decision to opt for the EPU difficult to understand.
One interpretation is that policy-makers' enthusiasm for the
payments union was misguided. Another, advanced in this
chapter, is that there in fact existed subtler obstacles to a quick
transition to convertibility. Early resumption would have con-
flicted with other fundamental objectives of policy, namely
concluding the domestic and international understandings
among interest groups and countries upon which the post-war
generation of European economic growth was based.

The Domestic Settlement

Post-World War II Western European growth was predicated
on a distinctive social pact, referred to in the literature on the
period as 'the post-war settlement.'[1] This was an attempt to
avoid repeating the disastrous aftermath of World War I. That
period had been marked by an intense struggle over income
distribution.[2] Fiscal systems had been fundamentally trans-
formed over the course of the war. Western European
countries had imposed comprehensive income and profits

taxes for the first time. Income and wealth had been redistributed wholesale by inflation, wage compression, and wartime garnishing of financial assets. The question for policy was whether to restore the status quo ante or to accept as permanent the changes which had occurred.

The dispute surrounding this question led to policy deadlock, labor militancy and capital flight, which disrupted post-war recovery and in extreme cases degenerated into hyperinflation. Unable to agree on the distribution of the national income, workers attempted to secure a larger share by pushing for higher wages. Capitalists passed wage increases through into higher prices. Unable to agree on a distribution of the fiscal burden, both groups resisted paying taxes. Governments financed the consequent budget deficits by printing money and issuing short-term debt, with predictable inflationary consequences.

After the second world war, a repetition of the debilitating struggle over income distribution that had characterized the post-World War I period was successfully averted. Workers agreed to wage moderation in return for management's agreement to reinvest the profits they thereby accrued in pro-ductivity-enhancing plant and equipment, rather than paying out profits as dividends. Each side agreed in effect to trade short-term gains for long-term benefits, so long as the other side agreed likewise.

In many European countries, workers consciously allowed real wage increases to lag behind productivity in order to provide incentives and resources for investment. In the Netherlands, for example, the unions agreed that the fruits of all productivity increases in the first half of the 1950s should be used to finance investment 'so that industry could earn profits which would pay for expansion and modernization of the productivity apparatus.'[3] In Germany, trade unions observed 'significant wage restraint' throughout the 'fifties.[4] Even in Britain, not renowned for labor/management harmony, the tripartism of World War II (regular consultation and cooperation between labor, management and government) survived into the post-war period. The Trades Union Congress cooperated with management and with the Conservative Governments that ruled from 1951 to moderate wage demands.[5] Industrial relations specialists like Solomon Barkin, in their explanations for the post-war boom, lay considerable stress on this growth-oriented consensus.[6]

Management, for its part, raised investment rates to nearly twice the level that prevailed before the war and to significantly higher levels than after 1972 when the post-war settlement began to unravel. Even in Britain, not one of Europe's high-investment countries, management agreed as part of the post-war settlement to restrain dividend payout and conspicuous consumption in favor of reinvestment, although this part of the bargain grew increasingly difficult to enforce following the return to office of Conservative Governments in 1951.[7] There may be grounds for criticizing British economic performance in the post-war period, but growth rates in the 'fifties were nonetheless impressive relative to preceding and subsequent decades.

Accompanying this high investment rate was rapid productivity growth. Even in Britain, the laggard, productivity growth rose sharply from 1924–37 to 1951–71, from 0.7 to 2.3 per cent per annum.[8]

Contemporary observers highlighted the importance of these trends for the post-war growth process. Henry Wallich (1955) emphasized the role of wage moderation in Germany in providing profits to be plowed back into investment, thereby sustaining productivity growth:

> 'For the economy as a whole labor's muted and unaggressive policy has been an inestimable advantage. It has, in the first place, made a major contribution *to the stability of the new currency* . . . in the second place, labor's restraint has helped to *make and keep exports competitive* . . . the final and probably most decisive contribution, however, has been to the *financing of the investment boom*. By allowing wages to lag behind profits, labor made it possible for business to engage in large-scale self-financing. The inequality of the income distribution favoring the higher incomes where proportionately more savings accrue, was the essential condition of the high rate of investment.'[9]

Figures 3 and 4 show that the point is general. Figure 3 displays the relationship between one measure of wage moderation (labor's share of income) and the national investment rates, confirming the Wallich hypothesis that countries with low labor shares had high investment rates.[10] Figure 4 shows that for this and other reasons emphasized by Wallich, low labor shares in the immediate post-war period tended to be associated with high growth rates.[11]

Reaching the settlement

There were two immediate conditions for achieving this settlement: first it had to be reached, and then it had to be sustained. Reaching it required minimizing the ratio of short-term sacrifices to long-term benefits, especially since discount rates were high in the immediate post-war years. With incomes and living standards still depressed, the marginal utility of consumption was high. Reaching an agreement that involved deferring consumption was unusually difficult. Indeed, it was

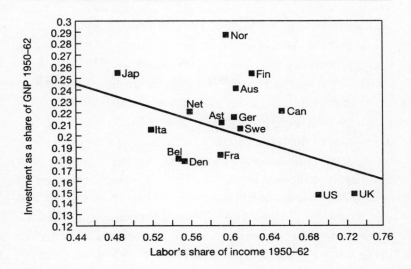

Figure 3 Investment rates and labor's share of national income, 1950–62.

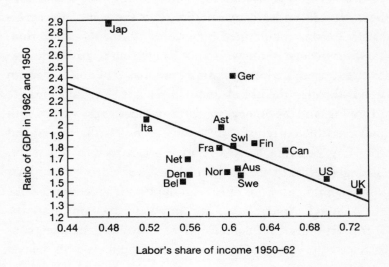

Figure 4 Economic growth and labor's share of national income, 1950–62.

only with the help of Marshall Plan transfers, which increased the size of the pie to be shared out among capital and labor, that it proved possible to strike this bargain at all.[12]

The EPU worked in the same direction by strengthening Europe's terms of trade, which moderated the requisite sacrifices in terms of living standards. Devaluation implied a worsening of the terms of trade, reducing the size of the pie to be shared out among competing interest groups. For devaluation followed by convertibility to balance the external accounts, residents of other continents had to be coaxed into purchasing more European exports, Europeans into purchasing fewer imports. A change in relative prices, namely a decline in the relative price of exports (a terms of trade deterioration), was needed to bring this about.[13]

Conversely, a payments union which restricted imports from extra-European sources, relative to how they would have been treated under convertibility, had the same effect as a tariff. Europe maintained balance of payments equilibrium *vis-à-vis* the rest of the world not by altering relative prices so as to export more but by limiting purchases of non-European goods through the use of import licensing, foreign exchange rationing, and the other administrative devices associated with inconvertible currencies. By reducing the European demand for US goods, this shifted relative prices in Europe's favor. Stronger terms of trade meant that fewer European exports could command more European imports from countries like the United States. As an implicit tax on imports, inconvertibility raised the level of European incomes consistent with balance of payments equilibrium *vis-à-vis* the rest of the world.

Opting for convertibility rather than the EPU would have shrunk European incomes by one to two per cent (the implication of the additional fifteen per cent devaluation identified in Chapter 3 as necessary for the restoration of external balance), an effect comparable to that of eliminating the Marshall Plan.[14] Workers would have voiced their objection by demanding higher wages to compensate for the reduction in real incomes, threatening the wage moderation evident in Table 11 (page 63). Firms would have attempted to pass through higher wages into higher prices, in turn eliciting further demands for wage increases. The fragile agreements between labor and capital over income distribution could have been threatened. As Thomas Balogh put the point for Britain,

> 'The import requirements from the US *at a tolerable standard of life* are far higher than dollar earnings. ... The drastic decrease in the standard of life needed to match US competition without discrimination *is politically so dangerous* as to be ruled out.[15]

Contemporaries emphasized these terms of trade effects. Arthur Smithies (1950) stressed that removing the quantitative restrictions associated with inconvertibility would require further devaluation, and that devaluation would entail terms of trade losses. A.C.L. Day (1953) similarly warned that the EPU countries would suffer terms-of-trade losses if they scrapped the payments union in favor of convertibility. The problem was summed up as follows by the OEEC in 1950: with European productivity growth lagging the American, 'the competitive position [the terms of trade] of Western Europe would deteriorate . . .' Attempting to rely on relative prices under convertibility, rather than the discriminatory measures permitted by a clearing mechanism, would lead to 'continuous pressure on the exchanges; a fall in the standard of living would be inevitable.'[16]

If governments and central banks refused to accommodate

the increased wage and price demands provoked by the deterioration in the terms of trade, unemployment would result. Policymakers in the Scandinavian countries were especially vociferous in their oppostition to convertibility on these grounds.[17] Convertibility would have entailed the adoption of deflationary policies. Absent the adjustment of wage demands, this implied unemployment. But such an outcome would have been unacceptable in the post-war political climate. 'There was no question of pressing on with deflation to the point of creating massive unemployment. It must be clearly understood that if the choice were between massive unemployment and the imposition of discriminatory restrictions, the latter would be preferred.'[18]

The British case, where the restoration of convertibility was contemplated in 1952–53, provides a revealing case study of these considerations. The Conservative Government that took over from Labour in October 1951 was faced with a weak balance of payments and steady reserve losses. Restrictive budgetary measures were one conceivable response. In addition, some of the government's economic advisors urged an exchange-rate adjustment to bring the balance of payments into line. They proposed restoring the pound's convertibility and allowing it to float downward as far as necessary to balance the external accounts. They argued that the exchange controls on which the EPU was based were too porous to withstand the overhang of sterling balances. Increasingly, Britain's inconvertible currency was being used to acquire goods in sterling markets for transhipment to markets willing to pay in dollars.[19]

Prime Minister Winston Churchill was drawn to the proposal to restore convertibility and let sterling float downward. But Lord Cherwell, his closest advisor, warned of the likely reaction of labor to the adverse impact on working-class living standards of the terms of trade deterioration that would be associated with depreciation. Given Britain's reliance on imported grain and other foodstuffs, the effect might be pronounced.

> If a 6 per cent Bank Rate, 1 million unemployed and a 2/- loaf are not enough, there will have to be an 8 per cent Bank Rate, 2 million unemployed and a 3/- loaf. If the workers, finding their food dearer, are inclined to demand higher wages, this will have to be stopped by increasing unemployment until their bargaining power is destroyed. This is what comfortable phrases like 'letting the exchange rate take the strain' mean.[20]

Ultimately these arguments carried the day. Abandoning the EPU for depreciation and a convertible pound was rejected. Restrictive budgetary measures and a higher discount rate were still required to balance the external accounts, but they were adopted under the aegis of the EPU, not convertibility and depreciation, thereby protecting the terms of trade in particular and the post war settlement in general.

As this episode makes clear, the need to protect the post-war settlement mitigated in favor of a payments union and against convertibility. The EPU, in this sense, was more than a device for reconstructing intra-European trade; its essential purpose was to facilitate selective intervention in domestic markets and to achieve external balance *vis-à-vis* the rest of the world at what Balogh referred to as 'a tolerable standard of life.'

Enforcing the contract

Once this bargain was struck, it still had to be enforced. In particular, a problem of time inconsistency had to be overcome. Labor had to be convinced to trade lower current compensation for higher future living standards despite intrinsic uncertainty over whether management would keep its part of the bargain – to reinvest the profits that accrued tomorrow as a result of labor's sacrifices today. This was a game with a second-mover advantage: having obtained concessions from the first mover (labor), the second mover (capital) could renege on the bargain, paying out profits rather than reinvesting. Awareness of this fact rendered labor hesitant to agree. Hence the maintenance of high investment and growth rates were threatened.[21]

Institutional arrangements to enforce the implicit contract and eliminate the time-consistency problem cemented the post-war settlement. Critical to the viability of the agreement were institutions designed to disseminate information and monitor compliance. The German system of workplace 'co-determination,' in which labor had input into managerial decisions, was only the most extreme example of the trend. In many countries, the representation of interest organizations on advisory and administrative committees of industry and government was made obligatory. Industry-level unions and employers associations exchanged information on the terms of their bargains through government-sanctioned peak associations.[22]

French initiatives are illustrative. Labor-management plant committees (*comités d'enterprise*) were established in the late 1940s. Law required such committees to be established in all enterprises employing fifty or more workers. Including elected representatives of the employees and delegates appointed by the employer or plant manager, the committees possessed consultative powers concerning production and economic decisions.[23] French labor-management relations were far from harmonious, but even there new institutions were established to carry out monitoring and information-dissemination functions.

In addition, governments helped to lock in the bargain through the adoption of programs and policies which acted as 'bonds' that would be lost in the event of reneging. They agreed to limit rates of profit taxation in return for capitalists keeping their part of the bargain and plowing earnings into investment.[24] They provided limited forms of industrial support (selective investment subsidies, price-maintenance schemes, orderly marketing agreements) to sectors that would have otherwise experienced competitive difficulties. Even in Germany, a bastion of free-market policies, an Investment Aid Law was passed in 1952 to subsidize investment in sectors which had contributed to the bargain by subjecting themselves to price controls.[25] Workers were extended government programs of maintenance for the unemployed, the ill and the elderly. In France, health, maternity, invalidity and old age insurance benefits were increased; family allowances were raised to much higher levels. Workmen's compensation was taken out of private insurance company hands and made part of the public system. This web of interlocking agreements functioned as an institutional exit barrier. As a commitment technology, it increased the cost of reneging on the sequence of concessions and positive actions that comprised the post-war settlement.

The EPU was an essential concomitant of these arrangements. Without the import licensing and foreign-exchange market rationing associated with it, which provided limited insulation from international competition, such intervention in the operation of domestic markets would have been much more difficult. More intense trade competition would have increased the budgetary cost of selective industrial subsidies. Preferential allocation of import licenses made this possible without direct budgetary outlays. More intense foreign competition would have made the degree of wage compression across sectors sought by 'solidaristic' trade unions more costly to effect. Social programs would have been threatened by pressure to minimize labor costs. For all these reasons, the web of institutional arrangements that provided the exit barrier would have been that much more difficult to spin. In the worst-case scenario, the domestic settlement might have broken down.

The International Settlement

The other element of the post-war settlement was rapid growth of trade in the context of European integration. Instead of reverting to the pattern of the 1930s, when national self-sufficiency had been cultivated at the expense of comparative advantage, post-WWII Europe exploited trade as an engine of growth. National economies were allowed to pursue their comparative advantage. Expanding the scale of the market allowed them to exploit economies of scale and scope.

This was accomplished in the first instance through the liberalization of intra-European trade. Quantitative restrictions on intra-European trade were removed more rapidly than those regulating transactions with other continents. There was a logic in relying on intra-European trade. The countries of Europe were natural trading partners for reasons of proximity and history. To say that Germany was a traditional exporter of capital goods and the other countries natural exporters of consumer goods is to generalize overly but to convey the essential point. Without a rapid expansion of trade to permit this pattern of comparative advantage to be exploited, it is doubtful that productivity and incomes could have risen as quickly as they did. And, as described above, slower growth emanating from the international sphere would have increased the sacrifices in living standards entailed in the domestic settlement, threatening that with breakdown as well.

Restructuring along export-oriented lines was costly. Before undertaking it policy-makers had to be convinced that Europe's free-trade commitment was permanent. Reallocating resources along lines of comparative advantage entailed sunk costs; it could be an expensive mistake if any of the major European trading nations reneged on its commitment to free trade.

Moreover, with memories of trade warfare in the 1930s still fresh, policymakers had to be convinced that the countries concerned – especially Germany – would make benign use of their increased productive capacity. The pessimistic view embodied in the Morgenthau Plan (after US Treasury Secretary Henry Morgenthau) was that two wars had proven that Germany could not be trusted to use its industrial capacity benevolently and hence should be pastoralized (forced to transform itself into a nation of small farmers). Permanently dismantling European industry, Morgenthau's opponents in the US State Department objected, would be to drill a hole through the heart of the European economy. A depressed Germany would drag down the demand for the exports of other European countries. Eliminating the continent's principal supplier of capital goods would artificially inflate the cost of investment throughout Europe, worsen the dollar shortage, and force other countries to divert resources away from their comparative advantage and into capital-goods production.[26]

For Germany, the *Wirtschaftswunder* required consent on

the part of the occupying powers that controls on the level of industrial production be removed. As a price for this, post-war policymakers required that Germany be integrated into the European economy and that credible barriers to exit be created to prevent that commitment from being reversed.[27] Germany, for its part required reassurance that its access to raw materials, industrial intermediates and foodstuffs produced abroad was guaranteed, given the prominence the Nazis had lent in the 1930s Germany's dependence on foreign supplies.

Germany's commitment to the removal of price controls and the liberation of market forces remained uncertain, it has been argued, as late as 1950.[28] Capital flight remained a problem, and the levels of production and investment needed to balance the external accounts were not forthcoming. The willingness of the US and other European countries to extend credits to Germany, and Germany's willingness to submit to the conditions with which those credits were associated, cemented the credibility of the Adenauer Government's stabilization and liberalization, finally unleashing the *Wirtschaftswunder*.

For those concerned to construct institutional barriers to exit, the EPU and the arrangements in which it was embedded were preferable to unilateral convertibility. Operating a payments union required a set of institutions (the Organization for European Economic Cooperation, which worked in tandem with the Bank for International Settlements) capable of monitoring compliance and imposing sanctions. EPU membership was linked to trade liberalization. Member countries committed under the terms of the agreement to 'the maintenance of desirable forms of specialization . . . while facilitating a return to full multilateral trade . . .'[29] The Code of Liberalization mandated a schedule of subsequent liberalizations. By February 1951, less than a year after the EPU went into effect, all existing trade measures were to be applied equally to imports from all member countries. Participants were required to reduce trade barriers by a given percentage of their pre-existing level, initially one half and then escalating to sixty and seventy-five per cent. The share of quota-free intra-European trade would rise to ninety per cent by the beginning of 1955. Countries failing to comply with this schedule or employing other policies to manipulate the terms or volume of their trade in undesirable ways could expect to be denied access to EPU credits.

The US Economic Cooperation Administration, which administered the Marshall Plan, supported the EPU. Hence, the leverage the US enjoyed as a result of the Marshall Plan served to further buttress the credibility of European countries' commitment to trade. Countries which failed to adhere to the international settlement risked losing their American aid.

Implications

In this light, the EPU emerges as critical for the reconstruction of Europe's trade. But it was not critical because the alternative of current account convertibility was infeasible technically. Rather, it was critical by virtue of its positive spill-overs for domestic and international political economy. These spill-overs in turn contributed importantly to the post-war growth process.

Two further elements are required for this argument to fall into place. First, evidence that the EPU was an effective means of discriminating against extra-European trade, a necessary condition for it to have had favorable terms-of-trade effects. Second, confirmation that these gains were not neutralized by other welfare-reducing distortions. It is to these issues that the next chapter turns.

Notes

1 Three recent instances where this concept is used are Middlemas (1986), De Long and Eichengreen (1993), and Broadberry (1993).
2 For additional detail on these issues, see Maier (1975) and Eichengreen (1992).
3 This is a quote from a union publication, cited in Windmuller (1969), pp.350–1. See also Abert (1969), pp.79–80.
4 See Maier (1984), especially pp.51–2.
5 For details, see Flanagan *et al.* (1983).
6 See Barkin (1983), especially pp.19–22.
7 Middlemas (1986), pp. 227–8 *et seq.*
8 These figures, based on estimates of the gross capital stock, are from Matthews, Feinstein and Odling-Smee (1982), Table 7.2.
9 Wallich (1955), pp. 299–300, emphasis added.
10 In this and the succeeding figure, 'Aus' denotes Australia, 'Ast' Austria. Clearly there is considerable dispersion around the regression line, with Norway and Switzerland behaving as prominent outliers. For a discussion of the unusual behavior of investment in Norway so evident in the figure, see Eichengreen and Uzan (1992).
11 The *Wirtschaftswunder* in Germany and the economic miracle in Japan stand out, in reflection of the fact that other factors also contributed to international variations in postwar growth performance. But even if these two countries are removed from the sample, a pronounced negative relationship remains between the two variables depicted in the figure: when Germany and Japan are removed from the sample, the t-statistic on labor's share in the regression line superimposed on the figure falls from 2.7 to 2.0.
12 The relevance of the Marshall Plan is emphasized by Casella and Eichengreen (1993), among others.
13 The regressions of Table 9 confirm that devaluation entailed terms-of-trade losses.
14 Imports were almost exactly 25 per cent of GNP in the participating countries. The standard formula (5% * 0.25) implies a 1.25 per cent fall

in real incomes.

15 Balogh (1949a), p. 238, emphasis added.

16 OEEC (1950), p. 217.

17 See Wexler (1983), p.165 and the references cited therein.

18 Harrod (1963), p. 122.

19 Cairncross (1992), p. 122.

20 Cited in Kaplan and Schleiminger (1989), p. 166.

21 This set of issues has been analyzed theoretically by Grout (1984) and van der Ploeg (1987). The latter's treatment is closest to the problem analyzed here. Both models show that higher investment rates can be sustained in the presence of implicit or explicit contracts that prevent the second mover from skimming rents.

22 See Lembruch (1984), pp. 68–72.

23 For details see Lorwin (1954), Chapter 7 and *passim*.

24 A detailed analysis of the construction of this bargain is provided by Middlemas (1986), especially Chapter 5.

25 Giersch *et al.* (1992), pp.82–3.

26 A useful review of this debate is provided by Gimbel (1976), especially Chapters 15–16.

27 This point is drawn from Berger and Ritschl (1993).

28 See Berger and Ritschl (1993).

29 Rees (1963), p. 123.

Chapter 6

Did the EPU have hidden costs?

A payments union, whatever its benefits, may also have hidden costs. One can imagine three related distortions to which such an arrangement can give rise. First, by encouraging trade among the members of the payments union but not with the rest of the world, it can be a source of trade diversion. Such a scheme, by providing credits for intra-union settlements but not for trade with other countries, can divert trade from low- to high-cost producers. Insofar as the EPU encouraged intra-European trade liberalization but not a commensurate reduction in barriers to trade with the rest of the world, the effect could have been reinforced.

Second, insofar as it discriminates against imports from the rest of the world, a payments union can be a source of relative price distortions. Goods which can be produced cheaply outside the union cannot be imported as freely as goods produced by other participating countries; by driving up the relative price of the former, the payments union may seriously distort the structure of prices.

Third, a payments arrangement under which participating countries maintain the inconvertibility of their currencies may make it difficult to borrow abroad. Uncertain about whether they will be able to repatriate their principal, potential foreign investors may hesitate to commit in the first place.

In fact, evidence of such distortions in the EPU years turns out to be weak. This points to the importance of special features of the policy environment and of the EPU itself that minimized negative side-effects.

Trade distortions

Even EPU enthusiasts like Triffin admit that the system 'entailed a certain degree of discrimination against non-EPU members.'[1] Participants could use import licensing and foreign-exchange rationing to discourage purchases of goods from nonmember countries. The liberalization provisions embodied in the agreement committed the participants to free their trade with other EPU members but allowed them to continue restricting imports from other countries. The governments of nonmember countries, notably the United States, were aware of the discriminatory nature of the EPU. The IMF similarly disapproved of the discriminatory implications of the arrangement.[2] But the Americans, for the same motives that lay behind the Marshall Plan, hesitated to object. As one influential commentator put it, 'so long as such a pronounced bias of world trade in our favor persists, we ought not to stand in the way of measures which may help to correct it.'[3]

Working in the same direction was the fact that credit was extended through the provision of EPU quotas to help countries finance their intra-union deficits, while deficits with the dollar area still had to be settled in gold. Moreover, repayments of accumulated EPU debts under the amortization schedules negotiated starting in 1954 could be used to finance intra-European trade but not trade with the dollar area. Thus, even after import licensing and foreign-exchange rationing were relaxed in the EPU's final years, the payments union still could have had discriminatory effects through the differential availability of credit.

One might question whether the EPU's discriminatory measures had teeth. Efforts to liberalize intra-European trade in the EPU's early years were less than completely successful. Governments were allowed to backtrack on these commitments in order to cope with balance of payments difficulties. Countries running perennial surpluses within the EPU were permitted to adopt discriminatory policies designed to limit their exports to other member countries.

Even if the EPU was discriminatory, its effects may have merely offset those of other trade distortions. European importers could presumably obtain trade credit from the US market but not from the credit markets of their European trading partners, which remained disorganized and controlled. The US Export-Import Bank, the Marshall Plan and subsequent US military aid subsidized imports from the dollar area.[4] In addition, the bilateral agreements under which Western European countries organized their trade with the rest of the world sometimes included credit ceilings even more liberal than those in the EPU agreement. The EPU's discriminatory provisions may have merely offset these effects, eliminating rather than spawning trade distortions.

Finally, one might go further and argue that the EPU was itself an active force promoting trade with the rest of the world. The commitment to trade liberalization embodied in the EPU agreement could have led European countries to liberalize their trade both within Europe and with the rest of the world more quickly than they would have otherwise, and more quickly than countries elsewhere freed their own international transactions. And by economizing on the use of reserves in settlements between EPU countries, the arrangement could have freed up reserves to finance additional trade *vis-à-vis* the rest of the world.

Whether the EPU had significant trade creating or diverting effects is ultimately an empirical question. To analyze it, I estimate gravity equations predicting the volume of bilateral trade flows for the first EPU year (1950), the system's mid-year (1954) and its final year (1958). The basic specification follows the work of Jeffrey Frankel (1992). The level of trade (exports plus imports), in log form, between country pairs is regressed on a measure of country size (the log of the product of the trading partners' GNPs), a measure of personal income (the log of the product of the trading partners' per capita GNPs), the log of the distance between the trading partners, and a dummy variable for contiguous countries.[5]

Population and national income data are drawn from the Heston-Summers International Comparisons Project data base, trade data from the UN's *Yearbook of International Trade Statistics*. The trade figures, expressed in domestic currency, are converted to dollars using Heston and Summers' purchasing power parity exchange rates so as to insure compatibility with the national income statistics.[6] A sample of thirty-six countries provides data on 620 bilateral trade flows.[7]

The equations are estimated by ordinary least squares.[8] The basic arguments of the gravity model all display their expected signs, as shown in Table 13. The coefficient on the product of per capita incomes, for example, ranges from 0.4 to 0.5, suggesting that trade increases with per capita income. Compared to the coefficient on this variable of 0.3 in the Frankel study, this suggests that the effect was stronger in the 1950s. The coefficient on the product of national incomes

Table 13 Determinants of trade in the 1950s
(t-statistics in parentheses)

Variable	1950	1954	1958	1950	1954	1958
Constant	−27.47	−30.54	−30.93	−27.48	−30.57	−30.95
	(21.98)	(22.81)	(21.02)	(21.96)	(22.83)	(21.06)
National Incomes	0.79	0.85	0.83	0.79	0.85	0.84
	(21.25)	(22.27)	(20.06)	(21.24)	(22.27)	(20.13)
Per capital incomes	0.40	0.47	0.50	0.39	0.47	0.49
	(6.86)	(7.50)	(7.21)	(6.61)	(7.35)	(6.89)
Distance	−0.10	−0.11	−0.13	−0.09	−0.11	−0.13
	(2.18)	(2.45)	(2.57)	(2.04)	(2.24)	(2.45)
Contiguous	0.91	0.86	0.83	0.89	0.96	0.92
	(3.38)	(3.12)	(2.70)	(3.15)	(3.32)	(2.87)
EPU	1.70	1.47	1.46	1.58	1.34	1.18
	(10.01)	(8.37)	(7.39)	(6.55)	(5.42)	(4.28)
Europe	–	–	–	0.17	0.11	0.31
				(0.74)	(0.46)	(1.16)
Western Hemisphere	–	–	–	0.02	−0.32	−0.36
				(0.07)	(1.34)	(1.36)
n	630	630	630	630	630	630
S.E.	1.414	1.453	1.615	1.416	1.453	1.613

Notes: Dependent variable is imports plus exports. All trade and income variables are expressed in US dollars, using the conversion factor described in the text.

ranges from 0.8 to 0.85, suggesting that trade increases less than proportionately with size. This compares with a coefficient of 0.75 in the Frankel study.

I first test the impact of the EPU on intra-European trade. This involves adding a dummy variable (denoted 'EPU') for when both trade partners were members of the payments union. The coefficient suggests a very considerable impact of the payments union on the level of intra-European trade. It declines slightly between 1950 and 1954 and again between 1954 and 1958, as if the hardening of EPU settlement terms and progressive removal of import controls under the provisions of the Code of Liberalization diminished its effect, consistent with the views of those who suggest that the effects of the EPU were most important in its early years.[9] Discrimination intensified in the early years, the coefficients suggest, as European countries liberalized their trade with other European countries more quickly than they liberalized trade with the dollar area. In the final EPU years, in contrast, trade with the US was liberalized relatively rapidly, and the terms of EPU settlements were hardened, in effect requiring the same payment terms for intra-EPU trade as for US trade.

One worries that the EPU coefficient is picking up the tendency for European countries to trade disproportionately with one another for reasons, such as history and geography, unrelated to the payments union.[10] Geographical factors should be captured to some extent by distance and contiguity. To be doubly sure that the EPU dummy was not picking up other continent-specific factors, I added additional dummy variables for European countries and for those in the Western Hemisphere.[11] In no year did either of these regional dummies differ significantly from zero at standard confidence levels. Nor did their inclusion alter the signs, relative magnitudes and statistical significance of the EPU variable.

As a test for trade discrimination, I added a second dummy variable (EPU-NON) for when only one of the two trade partners is a member of the clearing union. If the EPU was discriminatory, then the magnitude of EPU should be significantly larger than that on EPU-NON. The results of estimating this variant of the model are shown in Table 14. EPU is consistently larger than EPU-NON, and one can reject at the ninety-nine per cent confidence level the hypothesis that the two are equal to one another. EPU countries, in other words, traded significantly less with nonmembers than with fellow members, even after adjusting for the other standard determinants of trade. This is evidence that the EPU was discriminatory, and that the discrimination worked in the direction required by the terms-of-trade hypothesis of Chapter 5.

How should the positive coefficient on EPU-NON be interpreted? It is likely that it reflects in part the capacity of the EPU to economize on international reserves. Insofar as the payments union provided credits to finance intra-European trade, a lower level of reserves was required to offset fluctuations in that trade. A larger share of the reserves of European countries could therefore be used to support trade with the rest of the world. In other words, knowing that reserves were available to smooth fluctuations in dollar receipts, European countries were willing to incur a higher average level of current dollar obligations.

The positive coefficient on EPU-NON may also follow from the fact that the 1950s was the era of import substitution in other parts of the world. Following the collapse of trade in the 1930s, many countries in Latin America and other parts of the world adopted strategies of promoting domestic industrialization by restricting access for imported manufactures.

Table 14 Further determinants of trade in the 1950s
(t–statistics in parentheses)

Variable	Excluding Regional Controls			Including Regional Controls		
	1950	1954	1958	1950	1954	1958
Constant	-27.55	-30.52	-30.76	-27.51	-30.49	-30.74
	(22.46)	(23.51)	(21.34)	(22.48)	(23.47)	(21.30)
National incomes	0.80	0.86	0.85	0.80	0.86	0.85
	(21.87)	(23.29)	(20.78)	(21.92)	(23.25)	(20.77)
Per capital incomes	0.35	0.39	0.41	0.33	0.38	0.40
	(6.02)	(6.31)	(5.90)	(5.34)	(5.98)	(5.51)
Distance	-0.09	-0.10	-0.12	-0.08	-0.10	-0.11
	(2.04)	(2.29)	(2.43)	(1.81)	(2.18)	(2.23)
Contiguous	1.06	1.06	1.02	0.91	0.99	0.95
	(3.99)	(3.94)	(3.37)	(3.30)	(3.53)	(3.10)
EPU	2.11	2.01	1.97	2.21	2.10	1.86
	(11.34)	(10.57)	(9.10)	(8.38)	(7.83)	(6.14)
EPU-NON	0.63	0.83	0.76	0.74	0.89	0.79
	(4.98)	(6.40)	(5.23)	(5.36)	(6.32)	(4.95)
Europe	–	–	–	0.06	-0.02	-0.21
				(0.24)	(0.07)	(0.79)
Western Hemisphere	–	–	–	0.52	0.28	0.17
				(2.09)	(1.11)	(0.61)
n	630	630	630	630	630	630
S.E.	1.388	1.410	1.582	1.386	1.410	1.583

Notes: Dependent variable is imports plus exports. All trade and income variables are expressed in US dollars, using the conversion factor described in text.

The prevalence of tariffs and quotas sheltering infant industries continued to restrict the level of trade. The countries of Western Europe, in contrast, under US pressure, as formalized in the EPU Agreement itself, moved relatively quickly to restore access for imported goods, although, as described above, they liberalized intra-European trade significantly faster than trade with the rest of the world.

Price distortions

The possibility that inconvertibility distorted relative prices has been emphasized by previous authors.[12] One reason that the EPU could have fostered price distortions, they suggested, was the tendency for governments, enjoying the insulation afforded by currency conversion costs, to manipulate relative prices through the use of taxes and subsidies on domestic production. Equally important was the tendency for producers with market power to manipulate prices themselves. In France, for example, industrial agreements were formed in the industries producing gasoline, building materials, paper and cardboard, and nuts and bolts. In Italy, a commission set up to examine monopoly control and cartelization reported that concentration and inadequate competition existed in artificial silk, chemicals, engineering products, electric power, cement and rubber. In the UK, retail price maintenance agreements limited competition in the provision of glassware and dental goods, among other products. Cartels were prevalent in Swedish electrical goods, foundry products and paper, Swiss cement, chocolate, fats and oils.[13] This kind of imperfect competition at home meant that a system of inconvertible currencies that limited competition from abroad may have resulted in pronounced relative price distortions.

Systematically studying the deviation of relative price structures across countries before and after the EPU requires disaggregated price indices that are comparable internationally. The World Bank's International Comparisons Project provides disaggregated price indices for matched sets of more than thirty categories of goods and services for the US and the major European countries, but 1970 is the first year for which these data were assembled.[14] Fortunately, Milton Gilbert and Associates (1958), in an OEEC pilot study that preceded the World Bank project, provide comparable indices for 1950.[15] In Table 15 I compute a measure of the distance between relative prices in the US (which is taken as an indicator of undistorted world prices) and the corresponding price structure in each of the major European countries in 1950 and 1970. If that distance is larger in 1950 than in 1970, this confirms that exchange controls on merchandise transactions in the preconvertibility period were associated with relative price distortions.[16]

Table 15 does not indicate that the EPU distorted relative prices. As with any international comparison, how one deals with the index number problem has consequences for the results. When one uses European expenditure shares to weight the components of GNP, one finds that for two countries (the UK and Belgium) relative prices diverged from those of the US by more in 1950 than in 1970. For three countries (France, Italy and the Netherlands) they diverged by less in 1950, while for one country (Germany) there was essentially no difference across years. When US expenditure shares are used instead, Belgium's prices are no longer more distant from US prices in 1950 than in 1970, but otherwise the results are the same. That the UK is the one country whose relative prices consistently differed more from US prices in 1950 than in 1970 is

Table 15   Divergence of domestic price structures, 1950 and 1970

		Belgium	France	Germany	Italy	Netherlands	UK
Overall							
European } {	1950	3.71	0.97	1.08	5.74	0.87	1.49
Weights }	1970	3.53	1.45	1.12	6.05	1.00	1.31
US } {	1950	3.61	1.09	1.24	5.93	0.99	1.37
Weights }	1970	3.77	1.56	1.22	6.14	1.14	1.20
Consumption Goods							
European } {	1950	3.24	0.85	0.91	5.05	0.74	1.33
Weights }	1970	2.90	1.19	0.93	5.07	0.80	1.09
US } {	1950	3.17	0.96	1.11	5.17	0.86	1.16
Weights }	1970	3.13	1.32	1.04	5.10	0.95	0.96
Investment Goods							
European } {	1950	1.69	0.43	0.52	2.47	0.44	0.51
Weights }	1970	1.76	0.70	0.53	2.78	0.52	0.59
US } {	1950	1.59	0.62	0.47	2.53	0.47	0.50
Weights }	1970	1.60	0.49	0.52	2.70	0.47	0.62
Government Spending							
European } {	1950	0.63	0.18	0.21	1.17	0.09	0.42
Weights }	1970	0.99	0.42	0.32	1.78	0.31	0.44
US } {	1950	0.66	0.15	0.17	1.05	0.12	0.39
Weights }	1970	1.36	0.55	0.44	2.29	0.41	0.51

Note: Distance indicator calculated as $\sum_i \left([P_i - P_i^{US}]^2 S_i \right)^{1/2}$ where P is the log of the European price, P^{US} is the log of the US price, and S_i is the expenditure share of commodity i.

consistent with the fact that price controls were particularly pervasive there. But there is strikingly little evidence here that the EPU was a source of significant price distortions.

To understand why these results obtained, I computed the distance measure separately for three subcategories of national expenditure: consumption, investment and government spending. It turns out that the results for countries whose relative price structures are closer to US prices in 1950 than in 1970 are driven by public-sector spending. The government-spending category distinguishes compensation of public employees from expenditure on goods and services. The price of public-sector compensation is relatively low throughout much of Europe in 1950 and relatively high in 1970. Thus, the tendency for public-sector pay to rise relative to other prices in Europe over the two post-war decades contributed to the growing distance between the structures of US and European prices.

For the UK, the distance of relative consumption goods prices from US prices is greater in 1950 than in 1970 regardless of the weighting scheme, while it is greater for investment goods so long as US weights are applied. The large difference in the relative prices of consumption goods in 1950 reflects heavy taxes on items imported from the dollar area, such as tobacco. The difference in the structure of investment good prices reflects relatively high prices for producer durables and low prices for residential construction, a pattern consistent with the hypothesis that trade restrictions drove the relative price distortions. The tendency for Belgium's relative prices to differ more from US prices in 1950 than in 1970 (when European weights are used) reflects the behavior of the relative prices of consumption rather than investment goods. To cite two expenditure categories by way of example, fuel and transport services were heavily taxed, while the prices of bread and other essential foodstuffs were subsidized and controlled.

For most other countries the direction of the change between 1950 and 1970 remains sensitive to the weights employed. For them, even excluding the public sector there is no evidence of a systematic decline in the extent of relative price distortions between 1950 and 1970.

Thus, there is some evidence that inconvertibility and the associated import controls distorted the relative prices of consumption and investment goods in Britain (where control was relatively extensive) and, depending on the weighting scheme used, in Belgium. Overall it does not appear, however, that inconvertibility significantly aggravated price distortions.[17]

Distortions of capital flows

A third possible cost of inconvertible currencies under the EPU was discouragement of international capital flows. Unable to repatriate their principal and earnings so long as European currencies remained inconvertible, foreign investors would have remained unwilling to lend. As the United Nations explained in a report on post-war lending, many countries limited remittances of earnings, usually to a specified percentage of invested capital. Limitations on the outward transfer of principal were even more restrictive. The UN concluded that:

> Foreign enterprises are bound to feel the impact of such control in connexion (sic) with both the remittance of income (and the repatriation of capital, if desired) and the payment for imports required for operations. Exchange control is usually a symptom of balance of payments pressure; should the pressure increase, control may be tightened or the currency devalued. Either alternative, but particularly the former, may represent a powerful deterrent . . .[18]

Russell Leffingwell graphically portrayed the implications for one country, Britain

> There is not much reason to expect any great flow of money toward sterling now, such as occurred after 1919 and again after 1931 . . . As soon as the world became convinced after 1919, and again after 1931, that the free pound was undervalued, sterling attracted flight money, the money of speculators and investors all over the world, who bought the free pound cheap for a profit . . . Now, however, the pound is not

free, but is an inconvertible pegged currency, and foreign investors who hold sterling and sterling securities have had their investments frozen for years, and now devalued, and still can't get their money out.'[19]

Similarly, Giersch *et al.* suggest that an earlier restoration of convertibility would have attracted larger capital inflows into Europe, shortening the time needed for 'reconstruction and the partial catching up with the US.'[20]

Testing this hypothesis requires data on capital flows that are consistent over time and across countries. The IMF provides such data in its *Balance of Payments Statistics Yearbook*. These were gathered for all countries but the US, the principal international lender of the period, for which information was also available in *International Financial Statistics* on the economic determinants of capital flows. (Regressions including the US yielded essentially identical results.) The final sample included twenty-seven countries.

The format of the IMF data changes in 1959, although three years of retrospective data using the new format were also provided at that time. Given the difficulty of consistently comparing borrowing behavior across the change in format, two separate samples were constructed. The first covers EPU years (1952–8), when only Canada and Mexico of the countries in the sample had convertible currencies.[11] The second covers six years (1956–61) spanning the resumption of convertibility. (Convertibility was restored as of the beginning of 1959 in most of Western Europe and in Australia and New Zealand, and in Greece in 1960.)

The specification follows previous work on the determinants of borrowing by a cross-section of countries.[22] The dependent variable is the value of private capital flows in units of domestic currency.[23] A positive number denotes a capital inflow. Explanatory variables are nominal GNP, inflation, real economic growth, exports, and export variability (the standard deviation of exports over three years centered on the current one). A vector of dummy variables for years and for whether the currency was convertible are included as well.

The results, reported in Table 16, are remarkably consistent across periods and definitions of capital imports. The quantity of external borrowing is related negatively to exports, positively to export variability and, after 1955, negatively to country size as proxied by nominal GDP. In every case the dummy variable for convertibility is positive, as if convertible-currency countries had greater access to foreign capital markets, but it uniformly differs insignificantly from zero at standard confidence levels.[24]

This analysis yields no evidence, then, that the failure to restore convertibility before the end of 1958 had a significant impact on ability to borrow.

Minimizing Distortions

What was it about the design of the European Payments Union that minimized distortions? Consider first Europe's relatively high level of international trade. The obvious explanation for why the EPU did not depress Europe's trade with the rest of the world more dramatically is that the US made ongoing liberalization a condition for providing $350 million of working capital for the system and for the continued provision of Marshall aid. The preamble to the EPU agreement committed the participating countries to 'the maintenance of desirable forms of specialization . . . while facilitating a return

Table 16   Effects of convertibility on private external borrowing, 1952–61
(t-statistics in parentheses)

	1952–58 Private non-bank borrowing	1956–61 Private non-bank borrowing	1956–61 Private borrowing
Nominal GDP	0.01	–0.01	–0.01
	(0.57)	(4.31)	(5.10)
Exports	–0.10	–0.25	–0.27
	(3.49)	(7.75)	(8.89)
Export Variability	–0.21	–0.16	–0.11
	(2.22)	(1.33)	(1.02)
Inflation	37.65	59.70	52.60
	(0.39)	(0.41)	(0.39)
Real Growth	162.71	91.40	112.94
	(0.93)	(0.61)	(0.81)
Convertibility	2.38	0.92	3.64
	(0.09)	(0.03)	(0.13)
R^2	.26	.47	.54
Numbers of obs.	162	162	162

Notes: Dummy variables for years are included in all regressions but not reported. The inclusion of the vector of year dummy variables accounts for the absence of a constant term.

to full multilateral trade . . .' At the end of 1949, with US encouragement, the OEEC Council of Ministers agreed to abolish quantitative restrictions on fifty per cent of intra-OEEC trade within six weeks. (It is relevant that the OEEC had been founded in response to US demands that Europe create an international body to coordinate the dispersement of Marshall Plan aid.) It was agreed to precommit to a schedule of subsequent liberalizations that raised the share of quota-free intra-European trade to ninety per cent by early 1955. Various of these liberalization measures were extended to Europe's trade with other continents, especially after 1953.[26]

Less important but working in the same direction, the Marshall Plan and subsequent US aid stimulated both intra-European trade and Europe's imports from the rest of the world. Marshall aid was only loosely tied, as described in Chapter 2. Sometimes American administrators even expressed concern that Marshall-Plan-financed exports of goods in short supply domestically might hinder the expansion of the US economy and encourage aid recipients to import such goods from other sources.

For clarity, it is useful to mention three factors that do not appear to explain the positive coefficient on EPU-NON. First, US credit markets may have provided private finance for European trade. But there is no obvious reason that they would have provided more such credit for Europe than for other parts of the world, thereby stimulating trade between EPU and non-EPU countries relative to trade between pairs of non-EPU countries. Second, the US Export–Import Bank and kindred programs could have stimulated trade with the US relative to trade with other countries. I therefore added to the gravity equations a dummy variable for bilateral US trade flows but found that it displayed a small coefficient and a t-statistic of one or less. (None of the other coefficients or significance levels were noticeably affected.) Third, the Marshall Plan and post-Marshall Plan military aid could have stimulated imports by EPU countries. To test whether US aid stimulated imports by the recipient countries from the United States, I added a dummy variable for trade flows between EPU countries and the US but found that it too displayed a coefficient of zero.

Trade liberalization and aid-financed credits also help to explain the lack of price distortions. Marshall-Plan-financed imports of US goods limited the market power of European producers. And the liberalization of intra-EPU trade further diminished price distortions. If an individual European country freely imported a product line from the United States, forcing domestic prices to world levels, the freedom of intra-European trade tended to force prices elsewhere in Europe down to the same level. 'Intra-European trade liberalization often weakened, through transit trade and triangular transactions, the effectiveness of dollar discrimination itself.'[27] Even where imports from the US remained blockaded, the US was not always the lowest cost producer of particular goods. As noted by Triffin, 'for many categories of goods, the lowest European prices which [domestic producers] had to meet – Swiss prices for some goods, Belgian or German prices for others, etc. – were probably as competitive as those of any third country, including the United States.'[28]

Thus, as Triffin emphasizes, the fact that European countries traded extensively with one another allowed efficiency-enhancing arbitrage to operate powerfully, minimizing price distortions. And the fact that the economies of Europe, notwithstanding their troubles, possessed a number of world-class industries allowed intra-EPU trade to drive prices down to the levels established by the least-cost producer.

The absence of an impact on foreign borrowing is attributable in part to US policies designed to offset inconvertibility's effects. The US instituted a program to guarantee American foreign investments against the risk of inability to transfer funds. Pursuant to the Mutual Security Act of 1951 (the successor to the Marshall Plan), the government insured US investments against the risk of currency inconvertibility and loss through confiscation or expropriation. Individuals and companies investing in countries for which aid was authorized by the act (essentially, the former Marshall Plan recipients, plus Taiwan, Haiti, Israel and the Philippines) were eligible to participate. Through the middle of 1954, sixty-seven industrial investment guarantees

totaling $47.6 million had been issued to cover private invest-
ments. Of the total, $45.0 million insured against
inconvertibility of foreign currency assets.[29]

But the fact that the EPU failed to penalize participating
countries by significantly reducing their capital imports was
not attributable primarily to the structure of the payments
union agreement itself or to accompanying policies. The leg-
acy of interwar experience left no country, whether its
currency was convertible or not, in a position to attract
significant amounts of foreign capital in the 1950s.[30] Two-
thirds of the US foreign loans extended in the 1920s had lapsed
into default in the 1930s. Default even infected markets where
debts continued to be serviced. Defaults in one country
depressed the bond prices of its neighbors and interrupted
their access to international capital markets, as they under-
scored the special risks associated with international lending.

In the wake of World War II, private lenders remained
demoralized, and little private lending took place. As Herbert
Feis summarized the lenders' perspective,

> 'The great depression that began in 1929 brought our first
> great venture in foreign lending to a sick end. . . . It was gone,
> and seemingly for all time. . . . A general sigh of resolve was
> heard over the United States: Never again should we lend or
> invest our money in foreign lands.'[31]

In this climate, it mattered little for capital market access
whether or not countries restored currency convertibility.

Implications

The discriminatory features of the EPU emphasized by contemporaries do appear to have significantly affected the direction of international trade. Participants traded significantly

more with one another than would be predicted on the basis of their economic characteristics and the behavior typical of other countries. They traded significantly more with one another than they did with the rest of the world. These patterns presumably reflected the more rapid rate of liberalization of imports from fellow EPU members than from other countries, and the provision of credits to underwrite intra-EPU trade. Discriminatory measures of this sort were necessary to deliver the terms-of-trade benefits that were one of the EPU's attractions. At the same time, ancillary policies and fortuitous circumstances minimized the negative side-effects. The competitiveness of European producers, in conjunction with the high level of intra-European trade, minimized the damage from trade diversion and relative price distortions. US foreign investment guarantees and the relatively low volume of foreign portfolio investment that would have prevailed in the 1950s in any case for independent reasons meant that opting for convertibility would not have unleashed a surge of inward foreign investment. In this sense the EPU offered the best of both worlds.

Notes

1 Triffin (1957), p. 203. Circa 1954, Triffin himself estimated that the discriminatory provisions of the EPU led to a £650 million reduction in the demand for dollar imports. Cairncross and Watts (1989), p. 310. These authors cite a number of other contemporary estimates also based on the assumption of significant discriminatory effects.

2 See Rees (1963, p. 101 and *passim*) for details.

3 Williams (1949), p.443.

4 Aside from specified exceptions, the most important of which were described above, the procurement authorization requirements associated with its extension effectively barred the recipients from using Marshall aid to finance imports from other EPU countries.

5 Entering incomes in product form is suggested by modern theories of trade under imperfect competition (Helpman and Krugman 1985), which suggest that countries of similar incomes will trade more than pairs of very poor and very rich countries. For information on the construction of the distance measure, see Hamilton and Winters (1992).

6 Where UN trade data were expressed in dollars, it was necessary to first convert them back to domestic currency values using the market exchange rate. Since purchasing power parity exchange rates are not provided for Chile, market exchange rates are used instead.

7 The sample size does not equal thirty-six factorial because of missing observations. The countries are Morocco, Nigeria, South Africa, Canada, Mexico, the US, Argentina, Brazil, Chile, Colombia, Peru, Uruguay, Venezuela, India, Japan, Pakistan, Philippines, Austria, Belgium-Luxembourg, Denmark, Finland, France, West Germany, Greece, Ireland, Italy, the Netherlands, Norway, Portugal, Spain, Sweden, Switzerland, Turkey, the UK, Australia and New Zealand.

8 I also estimated the system of three equations for 1950, 1954 and 1958 using seemingly unrelated regressions. The estimates were virtually identical to those discussed in the text but for slightly smaller standard errors. Eichengreen and Irwin (1993) compare OLS (ordinary least squares) and Tobit estimates of gravity equations, showing that the choice of estimator does not have major implications for the results.

9 Rees (1963), p. 253; Kenen (1991), p. 258.

10 It might be thought that the positive coefficient on the EPU variable reflects the unusually rapid growth of the trade of the EPU countries in the 1950s due to the collapse of trade links during the war. But while this explanation might hold if the dependent variable was the rate of growth of trade, there is no obvious reason why it should find reflection in the level.

11 The EPU dummy differs from the Europe dummy by the exclusion of Spain and Finland and the inclusion of Turkey. An alternative specification would include Australia, New Zealand, Pakistan, South Africa and possibly Canada as EPU countries on the grounds that the system's operations covered all European transactions of the sterling area. Results of estimating this specification were virtually identical to those reported here. The only discernible difference was that the coefficient for pairs of EPU countries did not decline over time. In addition, to test whether the peculiar case of Germany, whose exports expanded enormously after 1949, dominated the results (see Chapter 3), I excluded the German observations from the sample. It turned out that

this did not alter the results significantly.

12 See for example Haberler (1954).

13 United Nations (1950), p. 103; Diebold (1952), pp. 284–5.

14 See Kravis, Heston and Summers (1978).

15 In a few instances the precise definition of expenditure categories differed across the two studies. In these cases it was necessary to combine adjoining categories to render the 1950 and 1970 data comparable.

16 Comparing 1950 with 1970 is likely to bias the results toward finding EPU-related price distortions. The trade equations just discussed suggest that the EPU was most restrictive in its early years. Similarly, trade liberalization proceeded throughout the 1960s under the aegis of the GATT (General Agreement on Tariffs and Trade), continuing to moderate price distortions as the decade progressed. Comparing 1958, the last EPU year, with 1959, the first year of convertibility, would presumably yield less evidence of distorting effects.

17 A possible objection to this conclusion is that the price data used in these international comparisons are not sufficiently disaggregated to pick up distortions to relative prices *within* expenditure categories. Unfortunately, more disaggregated data for 1950 do not exist. But to test whether higher levels of aggregation automatically bias the results in the direction of fewer price distortions in earlier years, I aggregated the thirty categories of expenditure available for both years into fifteen more encompassing 'super-categories.' Doing so had virtually no effect on the relative size of the distance measures in the two years.

18 United Nations (1954), p.54.

19 Leffingwell (1950), p. 209.

20 Giersch et al. (1992), p. 115.

21 Colombia and Venezuela are borderline cases with relatively modest programs of import licensing and otherwise convertible currencies. I replicated the analysis including them among the convertible-currency countries for all years and found that this did not alter the results.

22 The particular specification utilized here follows Riedel (1983).

23 The manner in which public borrowing is reported for some countries makes it difficult to distinguish foreign aid from commercial loans; this is one reason I concentrate on private borrowing. In addition, the IMF's pre-1958 format lumps together public and commercial bank borrowing; hence the precise definition of the dependent variable in this period is private non-bank borrowing.

24 As a further test, I related the *absolute value* of capital flows to these same variables. The results (not reported here) indicate that variable to

be significantly related to exports and export variability but insignificantly affected by convertibility.

25 Cited in Rees (1963), p. 123.
26 For details, see Wexler (1983), pp. 198–9 and *passim*.
27 See Triffin (1957), p. 207.
28 Triffin (1957), p. 207.
29 See US Congress (1953, 1954).
30 The evidence to this effect is analyzed in Eichengreen (1989).
31 Feis (1950), p. 1.

Chapter 7

Conclusions and policy implications

The institutions regulating international trade and payments tend to be dismissed as technical and obscure. This perhaps accounts for the small, specialized literature devoted to the European Payments Union. A central argument of this study is that relegating the EPU to the sidelines risks deflecting attention from the institutional arrangements upon which Europe's post-World War II growth miracle was based. By turning the terms of trade in Europe's favor, the EPU buttressed the contribution of the Marshall Plan, moderating the sacrifices in terms of living standards required to reach agreement on income distribution. Once this agreement was reached, macroeconomic stabilization could follow and with it decontrol and deregulation. This made possible the continued operation of market forces, sustaining economic recovery.

The particular bargain struck between labor and management in post-World War II Western Europe involved deferring current compensation in return for higher future incomes. Labor agreed that real wages might lag behind the growth of productivity to make profits available for investment. Management agreed to plow those profits into plant and equipment rather than paying them out as dividends. But institutional mechanisms were necessary to lend credibility to the bargain. In particular, labor had to be convinced that its current concessions in terms of compensation would really induce management to respond by increasing investment sufficiently to deliver productivity gains that would ultimately leave workers better off. Labor became convinced of this fact once the bargain was embedded in a network of institutional arrangements and policy concessions, all of which would have been jeapordized in the event that any party to the agreement reneged. Those institutional arrangements and policy concessions required government intervention in the economy – intervention that would have been more costly had the EPU not provided limited insulation from international competition. As a transitional arrangement phased out gradually through the hardening of settlements and eliminated once the other elements of the bargain could stand on their own, the EPU was ideally structured to support the post-war growth process. The EPU may have been only one small strand in the web of institutional arrangements holding the domestic bargain in place, but as such it provides a useful case study of forces at work.

The rapid productivity increases making immediate sacrifices palatable required nations to restructure their economies along export-oriented lines. In turn this required a mechanism to lend credibility to Europe's commitment to free trade and economic integration. Intra-European trade and payments were reconstructed not via a sequence of unilateral and potentially reversible decisions on the part of national governments to restore current account convertibility. Rather, trade and payments were liberalized through a coordinated process in which all the major European countries participated with the active support of the United States. The multilateralization of intra-European settlements was linked via the

Code of Liberalization to the reduction of barriers to trade. Institutional mechanisms like the EPU Managing Board, which worked in conjunction with the OEEC and the BIS, were created to monitor compliance. This created barriers to exit which rendered irreversible the commitment to trade liberalization and European economic integration, giving governments the assurance they required to restructure their economies along export-oriented lines. Internationally as domestically, the EPU was only one of several initiatives working in this direction; the European Coal and Steel Community is another example. Once again, however, the EPU serves as a useful case study of a general tendency.

Given this interpretation, is Western Europe's experience in the 1950s relevant for the FSU countries today? Can a payments union help cement the kind of domestic and international settlements upon which the golden age of post-war Western European growth was based? Or does the case for a FSU payments union rest narrowly on its capacity to provide multilateral clearing?

To be sure, a social pact comparable to that constructed in Western Europe after the war is desperately needed in the FSU countries today. The distributional struggle remains intense between competing claimants to shares of the national income. An agreement over income distribution that secured wage moderation and high investment would go a long way toward the resumption of economic growth. Insofar as the EPU helped to solidify the social compact upon which Western Europe's post-war growth was based, one might think that a payments union scheme could similarly help to defuse the struggle over distribution that debilitates policy in Russia and the other former Soviet republics today.

Unfortunately, the terms-of-trade benefits that helped the

EPU play its conciliatory role are not available to the FSU. Whereas the EPU countries accounted for more than a third of global industrial production in the 1950s, the members of a FSU payments union would account for very much smaller shares. They lack the market power to engineer a significant terms-of-trade improvement.[1] Neither is the rest of the world as prepared to accept terms-of-trade losses as was the United States in 1950. If the republics tried to use discriminatory trade policies to extract them, other countries might respond in kind. The terms-of-trade justification for the EPU in the 1950s hardly carries over to the 1990s.

Moreover, it is difficult to believe that a payments union scheme could put the finishing touches on social market economy and thereby lock in a distributional settlement in the FSU countries. Compared to post-World War II Western Europe, the gulf between competing distributional claims remains vast. The other elements of a distributional settlement are not yet in place. To support the nonexistent elements of a distributional settlement with a social market economy and that social market economy with a payments union would be putting the cart before the horse.

An international settlement among FSU countries akin to that achieved in Western Europe in the 1950s would be highly desirable. A credible agreement to liberalize intra-FSU trade and a commitment technology preventing countries from reneging would encourage the FSU countries to restructure along lines of comparative advantage and to continue exploiting the scale economies characteristic of the old system. But such agreements were locked in after World War II by the creation of European institutions whose short-run goal was deeper economic links and whose ultimate objective was political integration. These are precisely the kind of links that the former members of the Soviet Union are seeking to escape today. It seems implausible that a payments union scheme could be embedded in a broader framework that would lend it the same credibility-enhancing effects.

Thus, unlike the EPU, the case for a payments union for the FSU countries must rest narrowly on its capacity to provide multilateral clearing. Here the post-World War II precedent suggests that a payments union featuring credits will be viable only following macroeconomic stabilization. Prior to that, whatever credits are made available will be quickly absorbed by the countries where demand remains most out of control, perversely rewarding those countries with the worst domestic policies. Prior to stabilization, an FSU payments union with credits would suffer the same sad fate as the First Agreement on Multilateral Monetary Compensation and the Agreement for Intra-European Payments and Compensations.

If, following stabilization, the countries of the FSU opt for a payments union, it will be important to minimize the associated distortions. An important finding of this study concerns the market structures and policy initiatives that succeeded in doing so in the 1950s. The US, as underwriter of the payments union, had sufficient leverage to pressure the participating countries to liberalize their trade first with one another and then with the rest of the world. This, in conjunction with the fact that intra-European trade was extensive and European industries were relatively efficient, minimized price distortions. Investment guarantees played some role in minimizing capital market distortions.

It seems unlikely that these favorable conditions could be replicated in the FSU today. Few former-Soviet industries are world class; in this sense intra-FSU trade will be a poor substitute for trade with the rest of the world. This introduces more scope for trade diversion and relative price distortions insofar as any payments union has a discriminatory element. The West is likely to have less capacity to influence the international economic policies of the Soviet Union's successor states than did the US over Western Europe after World War II, whether or not it underwrites the operation of an FSU payments union and provides extensive foreign aid.

For all these reasons, arrangements for the international trade and payments of the FSU countries will necessarily depart from the precedent of the EPU. Based on a close study of its history, this should not be surprising. Economic and political conditions in post-war Western Europe were distinctive in important ways, a fact which mandated a policy response tailored to the circumstances. The same is true today.

Notes

1 Concentrating on overall trade shares may neglect these countries' market power in individual commodities. The significant exception to the generalization may be Russian exports of petroleum. But an oil export tax, like that currently imposed, would be sufficient to capture any potential terms of trade gains without necessitating a payments union scheme.

Further analysis of the 1949 devaluations

A possible reservation about Chapter 3's cross-section analysis of the effects of exchange-rate changes on the external accounts is that it fails to control adequately for other determinants of imports, exports and the terms of trade. In this appendix, I therefore provide a pooled time-series cross-section analysis which provides adequate degrees of freedom for analyzing such additional determinants.

I use annual data for the period 1949–1955, drawn from the sources described in Eichengreen and Uzan (1992). The sample of countries is the same as in Chapter 3, except that Greece, Ireland, Luxembourg, Portugal and Turkey are omitted because of the unavailability of information on one or more of the ancillary variables.

Regressions explaining the change in export volumes, import volumes and the terms of trade are shown in Table 17. These should be thought of as reduced forms of the underlying simultaneous supply-demand system. Along with the change in the nominal exchange rate and a vector of dummy variables for years, explanatory variables include population growth, the rate of consumer price inflation, the growth rate of industrial production, and openness (exports as a share of GNP). In alternative versions of the equations, a dummy variable for

Table 17 Estimated effects of exchange rate changes 1949–55
(Pooled time-series cross-section analysis)
(t-statistics in parentheses)

Explanatory Variable	Change in Exports		Change in Imports		Change in Terms of Trade	
Constant	-0.83	-0.78	0.29	0.30	1.28	1.28
	(5.08)	(4.99)	(2.57)	(2.67)	(16.69)	(16.52)
Change in exchange rate	0.85	0.81	-0.26	-0.27	-0.29	-0.29
	(5.51)	(5.50)	(2.49)	(2.58)	(3.95)	(3.94)
Population growth	0.26	-0.02	-0.62	-0.68	-0.72	-0.74
	(0.15)	(0.01)	(0.51)	(0.56)	(0.86)	(0.87)
Inflation	-0.87	-0.49	-0.36	-0.27	0.27	0.03
	(2.81)	(1.53)	(1.73)	(1.18)	(1.88)	(1.86)
Output growth	1.09	0.64	1.10	0.99	0.10	0.07
	(5.17)	(2.52)	(6.35)	(4.90)	(0.80)	(0.50)
Openness	-0.05	-0.01	0.06	0.07	0.04	0.05
	(0.43)	(0.08)	(0.73)	(0.86)	(0.79)	(0.82)
Germany	–	0.18	–	0.05	–	0.01
		(2.98)		(1.07)		(0.35)
Standard error	0.124	0.118	.085	.085	.058	.058
Number of Obs.	84	84	83	83	83	83

Notes: All equations include dummy variables for years.
Source: see text.

Germany is added as in Chapter 3 above.

The first two columns show the results for exports. The nominal exchange rate has a highly significant effect on exports, with point estimates a bit larger than those found in the cross-section analysis reported in the text. Two additional variables have statistically significant effects: countries in which industrial production expanded rapidly experienced unusually rapid export growth, while countries with relatively high domestic inflation exported less (as if their exports were priced out of international markets).

The next pair of columns show analogous results for imports. Once again the coefficient on the nominal exchange rate differs significantly from zero at the ninety-five per cent confidence level. The magnitude of the coefficient is essentially the same as in the cross-section analysis in the text. Again it appears that rapidly growing countries imported more but that countries with relatively high inflation rates imported less.

The final columns report the results for the terms of trade. The nominal exchange rate is significant at the ninety-nine per cent confidence level, and it displays a coefficient very similar to that in the main text. The only other variable with a significant effect is domestic inflation, confirming that countries with rapid inflation not offset by exchange-rate depreciation enjoyed an improvement in their terms of trade.

Thus, the results here verify the implications of the cross-section analysis in the text. While documenting that other variables such as growth and inflation also influenced the evolution of the trade balance, they provide additional support for the estimates reported in Chapter 3.

References

Abert, J. G. (1969), *Economic Policy and Planning in the Netherlands*, New Haven, Yale University Press.

Armstrong, P. A. Glyn and J. Harrison (1991), *Capitalism Since 1945*, Oxford, Blackwell.

Balogh, T. (1949a), 'Should sterling be devalued?' *Bulletin of the Oxford University Institute of Statistics*, 11, 228–52.

Balogh, T. (1949b), *The Dollar Crisis: Causes and Cure*, Oxford, Blackwell.

Balogh, T. 'The international aspect', in G. D. N. Worswick and P. H. Ady (eds), *The British Economy 1945–1950*, Oxford, Clarendon Press, 1954.

Bank for International Settlements, *Annual Report*, Basle, BIS, various years.

Barkin, S. 'The post-war decades: growth and activism followed by stagnancy and malaise', in S. Barkin (ed.), *Worker Militancy and its Consequences*, New York, Praeger, 1983.

Bean, R. W. (1948), 'European multilateral clearing', *Journal of Political Economy*, 56, 403–15.

Berg, A. and J. Sachs (1992), 'Stabilizing a previously centrally planned economy: the case of Poland', *Economic Policy*, 14, 117–74.

Berger, H. and A. Ritschl (1993), 'Germany and the political economy of the Marshall Plan', 1947–1952: a re-revisionist view', in B. Eichengreen (ed), *Europe's Postwar Growth, Revisited* (forthcoming).

Bernstein, E. M. (1948), *Latent inflation: problems and policies*, Staff Memorandum 221, April, Washington, DC, International Monetary Fund.

Blancpain, J. P. (1962), *Vom Bilateralismus zur Konvertibilität*, Zürich, Buch und Offsetdruck Stanz & Co.

Bofinger, P. and D. Gros (1992). 'A multilateral payments union for the Commonwealth of Independent States: why and how?' CEPR Discussion Paper 654.

Bossuat, G. (1992), *La France, l'aide américaine et la construction européene 1944–54*, Paris, Imprimerie Nationale, 1992.

Broadberry, S. (1993), 'Why was unemployment in post-war Britain so low?' CEPR Discussion Paper 541, in D. McCloskey and R. Floud, (eds), *The Economic History of Britain Since 1700*, 2nd edition, Cambridge, Cambridge University Press, forthcoming.

Buchheim, C. (1990), 'Monetary integration of Eastern Europe into the world economy', Munchener Wirtschaftswissenschaftliche Beitrage 5.

Cairncross, A. (1985), *Years of Recovery*, London, Methuen.

Cairncross, A. (1992), *The British Economy Since 1945*, Oxford, Blackwell.

Cairncross, A. and N. Watts (1989), *The Economic Section 1939–1961: A Study in Economic Advising*, London, Routledge.

Capie, F. and A. Webber (1985), *A Monetary History of the United Kingdom, 1870–1982*, London, Allen & Unwin.

Casella, A. and B. Eichengreen (1993), 'Halting inflation in Italy and France after World War II', in M. Bordo and F. Capie, (eds), *Monetary Regimes in Transition*, Cambridge, Cambridge University Press, forthcoming.

Clark, C. (1949), 'The value of the pound', *Economic Journal*, LIX, 198–207.

Collins, S. and D. Rodrik (1991), *Eastern Europe and the Soviet Union in the World Economy*, Washington, DC, Institute for International Economics.

Dam, K. W. (1982), *The Rules of the Game*, Chicago, University of Chicago Press.

Daviddi, R. and E. Espa (1992), 'Foreign aid and payments agreements in Central and Eastern Europe', *Economic Notes*, 21, 15–38.

Day, A. C. L. (1953), 'Convertibility and the European Payments Union', *Oxford Bulletin of Economics and Statistics*, 15, 151–62.

Day, A. C. L. (1954), *The Future of Sterling*, Oxford, Clarendon Press.

De Long, J. B. and B. Eichengreen, 'The Marshall Plan: history's most successful structural adjustment program', in R. Dornbusch *et al.* (eds), *Postwar Economic Reconstruction and Lessons for the East Today*, Cambridge, MIT Press, pp. 189–230.

Dickhaus, M. (1992), 'German attitudes toward the post-war payments systems: costs and benefits of regional payments cooperation', unpublished manuscript, European University Institute.

Diebold, W. (1952), *Trade and Payments in Western Europe: A Study in Economic Cooperation, 1947–51*, New York, Harper and Row.

Dooley, M. (1992), 'A payments mechanism for the Independent States of the Former Soviet Union', unpublished manuscript, University of California at Santa Cruz.

Dornbusch, R. (1974), 'Real and monetary aspects of the effects of exchange-rate changes', in R. Z. Aliber, (ed.), *National Monetary Policies and the International Financial System*, Chicago, University of Chicago Press, 1974, pp. 64–81.

Dornbusch, R. (1992), 'A payments mechanism for the Soviet Union and Eastern Europe', in D. Gros, J. Pisani-Ferry and A. Sapir, (eds), *Interstate Economic Relations in the Former Soviet Union*, Brussels, Centre for European Policy Studies, pp. 31–40.

Dornbusch, R. and H. Wolf (1990), 'Monetary overhang and reforms in the 1940s', NBER Working Paper 3456.

Dow, C. (1964), *The Management of the British Economy, 1945–1960*, Cambridge, Cambridge University Press.

Drabek, Z. (1992), 'Convertibility or a payments union? Convertibility!' in J. Flemming and J. M. C. Rollo, (eds), *Trade and Payments Adjustment in Central and Eastern Europe*, London, Royal Institute of International Affairs and European Bank for Reconstruction and Development, pp. 57-74.

Economic Cooperation Administration, Special Mission to the UK (1951), *The Sterling Area*, London, ECA.

Eichengreen, B. (1989), 'The US capital market and foreign lending, 1920–55', in J. Sachs (ed), *Developing Country Debt and Economic Performance, 1: The International Financial System*, Chicago, University of Chicago Press, pp. 107–55.

Eichengreen, B. (1990), 'The gold-exchange standard and the Great Depression', in B. Eichengreen, *Elusive Stability: Essays in the History of International Finance 1919–1939*,

Cambridge, Cambridge University Press, pp. 239–70.

Eichengreen, B. (1992), *Golden Fetters: The Gold Standard and the Great Depression, 1919–1939*, New York, Oxford University Press.

Eichengreen, B. and D. Irwin (1993), 'Trade blocs, currency blocs and the reorientation of trade in the 1930s', unpublished manuscript, University of California at Berkeley and University of Chicago.

Eichengreen, B. and J. Sachs (1985), 'Exchange rates and economic recovery in the 1930s', *Journal of Economic History*, 45, 925–46.

Eichengreen, B. and M. Uzan (1992), 'The Marshall Plan: economic effects and implications for Eastern Europe and the former USSR', *Economic Policy*, 14, 13–76.

Emminger, O. (1951), 'Die Europaische Zahlungsunion als Etappe der Europäischen Währungs-Neuordnung', *Zeitschrift für die gesamte Staatswissenschaft*, 107, 605–59.

Erhard, L. (1954), *Deutschlands Rückkehr zum Weltmarkt*, Düsseldorf, Econ-Verlag, 2nd edition.

Ethier, W. J. (1990), 'Proposal for an Eastern European payments union', unpublished manuscript, University of Pennsylvania.

European Payments Union (1951), *Report of the Managing Board*, Paris: OEEC.

Feinstein, C. (1972), *National Income, Expenditure and Output of the United Kingdom, 1855–1965*, Cambridge, Cambridge University Press.

Feis, H. (1950), *The Diplomacy of the Dollar, First Era, 1919–1932*, Baltimore, Johns Hopkins University Press.

Flanagan, R. J., D. W. Soskice and L. Ulman (1983), *Unions, Economic Stabilization, and Incomes Policies*,

Washington, DC, The Brookings Institution.

Flood, R. and P. Garber (1984), 'Collapsing exchange-rate regimes: some linear examples', *Journal of International Economics*, 17, 1984, pp. 1–13.

Frankel, J. A. (1992) 'Is Japan creating a yen bloc in East Asia and the Pacific?' NBER Working Paper 4050.

Friedman, M. (1953), 'The case for flexible exchange-rates', in M. Friedman, *Essays in Positive Economics*, Chicago, University of Chicago Press, pp. 157–203.

Giersch, H. K.-H. Paque and H. Schmieding (1992), *The Fading Miracle: Four Decades of Market Economy in Germany*, Cambridge, Cambridge University Press.

Gilbert, M. and Associates (1958), *Comparative National Products and Price Levels*, Paris, OEEC.

Gimbel, J. (1976), *The Origins of the Marshall Plan*, Stanford, Stanford University Press, 1976.

Glyn, A. A. Hughes, A. Lipietz and A. Singh (1990), 'The rise and fall of the golden age', in S. Marglin and J. Schor, (eds), *The Golden Age of Capitalism: Reinterpreting the Postwar Experience*, Oxford, Clarendon Press, pp. 39–125.

Gros, D., (1993) 'The Interstate Bank: An end to monetary disintegration in the former Soviet Union', unpublished manuscript, CEPS.

Grout, P. A. (1984), 'Investment and wages in the absence of binding contracts: A Nash bargaining approach', *Econometrica*, 52, 449–60.

Haberler, G., (1954), 'Konvertibilität der währungen', in G. Haberler et al., *Die Konvertibilität der Europaischen Währungen*, Zürich, Eugen Rentsch Verlag, pp.13–59.

Hall, M. (1950), 'The United Kingdom after devaluation', *American Economic Review*, XL, 864–75.

Hamilton, C. and A. Winters (1992), 'Opening up international trade with Eastern Europe', *Economic Policy*, 14, 77–117.

Hardt, J. P. (1990), 'The Soviet economy in crisis and transformation', unpublished manuscript, NATO Economic Colloquium.

Harrod, R. (1963), *The Dollar*, New York, Norton, 3rd edition.

Hawtrey, R. (1953), 'Confidence and convertibility', *International Affairs*, 29, 429–38.

Helpman, E. and P. Krugman (1985), *Market Structure and Foreign Trade*, Cambridge, Mass., MIT Press.

Hirschman, A. O. (1949), 'Devaluation and the trade balance', *Review of Economics and Statistics*, 31, 1949, 50–3.

International Monetary Fund (various years), *Balance of Payments Yearbook*, Washington DC, IMF.

International Monetary Fund (various years), *International Financial Statistics*, Washington, DC, IMF.

Jack, D. J. (1927), *The Restoration of European Currencies*, London, P. S. King.

Jacobsson, P. (1951), 'Monetary improvements in Europe and problems of a return to convertibility', *National Bank of Egypt Fiftieth Anniversary Commemoration Lectures*, Cairo, National Bank of Egypt.

Jacobsson, P. (1954), 'The Problem of Convertibility for Western Europe', *International Affairs*, 30, 137–47.

Kaplan, J. J. and G. Schleiminger (1989), *The European Payments Union: Financial Diplomacy in the 1950s*, Oxford, Clarendon.

Kenen, P. B. (1991), 'Transitional arrangements for trade and payments among CMEA countries', *Staff Papers*, 38, 235–67.

Kent, T. W. (1950), 'Devaluation one year after', *Lloyds Bank Review*, Oct., 22–37.

Kindleberger, C. P. (1950), *The Dollar Shortage*, London, Chapman & Hall.

Kindleberger, C. P. (1984), *A Financial History of Western Europe*, Winchester, Mass., Allen & Unwin.

Kornai, J. (1990), *The Road to a Free Economy*, New York, Norton.

Kravis, I. B., A. Heston and R. Summers (1978), *International Comparisons of Real Product and Purchasing Power*, Baltimore, Johns Hopkins.

Krugman, P. (1979), 'A model of balance of payments crises', *Journal of Money, Credit and Banking*, 11, 1979, 311–25.

Krugman, P. and M. Miller, (eds) (1991), *Target Zones and Currency Bands*, Oxford, Oxford University Press.

Lavigne, M. (1990), 'Economic relations between Eastern Europe and the USSR: bilateral ties vs. multilateral cooperation', unpublished manuscript, NATO Economic Colloquium.

League of Nations, *Monetary Review*, Geneva, League of Nations, various years.

League of Nations, *Monthly Bulletin of Statistics*, Geneva, League of Nations, various years.

Leffingwell, R. C. (1950), 'Devaluation and European recovery', *Foreign Affairs*, 37, 203–14.

Lembruch, G. (1984), 'Concertation and the structure of corporatist networks', in J. H. Goldthorpe (ed.), *Order and Conflict in Contemporary Capitalism*, Oxford, Clarendon Press, pp. 60–80.

Lorwin, V. R. (1954), *The French Labor Movement*, Cambridge, Mass., Harvard University Press.

Maier, C. (1975), *Recasting Bourgeois Europe*, Princeton,

Princeton University Press.

Maier, C. (1984), 'Preconditions for corporatism', in J. H. Goldthorpe, (ed.), *Order and Conflict in Contemporary Capitalism*, Oxford, Clarendon Press, pp. 39–59.

Maier, C. (1987), 'The two post-war eras and the conditions for stability in twentieth-century Western Europe', in C. Maier, *In Search of Stability*, Cambridge, Cambridge University Press, pp. 153–84.

Matthews, R.C.O., C. Feinstein and J. Odling Smee (1982), *British Economic Growth, 1865–1973*, Stanford, Stanford University Press.

Meade, J. (1953), 'The convertibility of sterling', *Three Banks Review*, 19, 3–26.

Michalopoulos, C. and D. Tarr (1993), 'Trade and payments among the successor states of the USSR', unpublished manuscript, The World Bank.

Middlemas, K. (1986), *Power, Competition and the State, 1: Britain in Search of Balance, 1940–61*, London, Macmillan.

Milward, A. (1984), *The Reconstruction of Western Europe, 1945–1951*, London, Methuen.

Mitchell, B. R. (1926), *European Historical Statistics*, London, Macmillan.

Mitchell, B. R. (1983), *International Historical Statistics*, London, Macmillan.

Newbery, D. and P. Kattuman (1992), 'Market concentration and competition in Eastern Europe', CEPR Discussion Paper 664.

Nurkse, R., (1944), *International Currency Experience*, Geneva, League of Nations.

Nurkse, R. (1953), 'The problem of currency convertibility today', *American Economic Review*, XXV, 321–38.

OECD (1990), *Economic Outlook*, June, Paris, OECD.

OEEC (various years), *Statistical Yearbook*, Paris, OEEC.

OEEC (1950), *European Recovery Program: Second Report of the OEEC*, Paris, OEEC.

OEEC (1954), *Statistics of National Product and Expenditure, 1*, Paris, OEEC.

OEEC (1957), *Statistics of National Product and Expenditure, 2*, Paris, OEEC.

Orcutt, G. H. (1950), 'Measurement of Price Elasticities in International Trade', *Review of Economics and Statistics*, XXXII, 117–32.

Polak, J. J. (1953), 'Contribution of the September 1949 devaluations to the solution of Europe's dollar problem', *Staff Papers*, 2, 1–32.

Polak, J. J. (1991), 'Currency convertibility in Eastern Europe: an indispensable element in the transition process', in John Williamson, (ed.), *Currency Convertibility in Eastern Europe*, Washington, DC, Institute for International Economics, pp. 21–30.

Rees, G. L. (1963), *Britain and the Postwar European Payments Systems*, Cardiff, University of Wales Press.

Riedel, J. (1983), 'Determinants of LDC borrowing in international financial markets: theory and empirical evidence', unpublished manuscript, The World Bank and Johns Hopkins University.

Robbins, L. (1947) 'Inquest on the crisis', *Lloyds Bank Review*, Oct., 1–27.

Schmieding, H. (1992), 'No need for a monetary halfway house: lessons from the European Payments Union for Post-Soviet currency arrangements', Kiel Discussion Paper 189, Aug.

Smithies, A. (1950), 'European unification and the dollar problem', *Quarterly Journal of Economics*, **XLIV**, 159–82.

Soros, G. (1990), *Opening the Soviet System*, London, Weidenfelt and Nicolson.

Statist (1951), 'Improvement in the Dutch currency position', *The Statist*, Oct., 540–1.

Statist (1953), 'Could European currencies be made convertible forthwith?' *The Statist*, Oct., 520–1.

Statist, (1954), 'Adequate reserves for convertibility', *The Statist*, April, 462–3.

Tew, B. (1965), *International Monetary Co-operation, 1945–65*, 8th edition, London, Hutchinson.

Tew, B. (1988), *The Evolution of the International Monetary System, 1945–88*, London, Hutchinson, 1988.

Tew, B. (1991), 'Then and now: trade and payments in Western Europe in the 1950s and in Eastern Europe in the 1990s', unpublished manuscript, United Nations.

Triffin, R. (1957), *Europe and the Money Muddle*, New Haven, Yale University Press.

United Kingdom, HM Treasury (1959), *United Kingdom Balance of Payments 1946–1957*, London, HMSO.

United Nations (1954), *The International Flow of Private Capital 1946–1952*, New York, United Nations.

United Nations (various years), *Yearbook of International Trade Statistics*, Geneva, United Nations.

United Nations (various years), *Statistical Bulletin*, Geneva, United Nations.

United Nations, Economic Commission for Europe (1948), *A Survey of the Economic Situation and Prospects of Europe*, Geneva, United Nations.

United Nations, Economic Commission for Europe (1950), *Economic Survey of Europe in 1948*, Geneva, United Nations.

United Nations, Economic Commission for Europe (1951), *Economic Survey of Europe in 1949*, Geneva, United Nations.

United Nations, Economic Commission for Europe (1951), *Economic Survey of Europe in 1950*, Geneva, United Nations.

United Nations, Economic Commission for Europe (1990), *Economic Survey of Europe, 1989–90*, Geneva, United Nations.

Urquhart, M. C. and K. A. H. Buckley (1965), *Historical Statistics of Canada*, Cambridge, Cambridge University Press.

US Congress (1953), *Report to Congress on the Mutual Security Program for the Six Months Ended June 30, 1953*, Washington, DC, GPO.

US Congress (1954), *Report to Congress on the Mutual Security Program for the Six Months Ended June 30, 1954*, Washington, DC, GPO.

US Department of Commerce (1976), *Historical Statistics of the United States*, Washington, DC, US GPO.

van Brabant, J. (1990), 'Convertibility in Eastern Europe through a payments union', unpublished manuscript, Institute for International Economics.

van Brabant, J. (1991), 'A multilateral payments union for Eastern Europe? A comment', *Banca Nationale del Lavoro Quarterly Review*, 176, 89–97.

van der Ploeg, F. (1987), 'Trade unions, investment and employment: a non-cooperative approach', *European Economic Review* 31, 1465–92.

Wallich, H. (1955), *Mainsprings of the German Revival*, New Haven, Yale University Press.

Wexler, I. (1983), *The Marshall Plan Revisited*, Westport,

Connecticut, Greenwood Press.

Williams, J. H. (1949), 'Europe after 1952', *Foreign Affairs*, 27, 426–48.

Williamson, J. (1992), *Trade and Payments After Soviet Disintegration*, Policy Analyses in International Economics, 37, Washington, DC, Institute for International Economics.

Windmuller, J. P. (1969), *Labor Relations in the Netherlands*, Ithaca, NY, Cornell University Press.

Index